LIFE AMONG THE DEAD

by

Michael Jack

Foreword by
The Rt. Rev. The Lord Coggan D.D.

CORTNEY PUBLICATIONS LUTON

Published in 1981
by
Cortney Publications
95-115 Windmill Road, Luton, Beds.

ISBN 0 904378 15 2

Cover Design by E.T. Davies

Printed in Great Britain by
INPRINT OF LUTON (Designers & Printers) LIMITED
95-115 Windmill Road, Luton, LU1 3XS

What the book is about

Basically this book is about a man and his deafness and how he has coped with his disability since birth. There are digressions which reflect the author's varied interests, which include music, photography, local history, underground exploration, journalism, and parapsychology.

Faced with earning a living after the failure of a farming venture, the author started a grass cutting business specialising in the maintenance of churchyards, which has kept him fully occupied for nearly thirty years. In addition to caring for between 30 and 40 churchyards he also looks after forty-five or so local lawns, single handed.

Compelled to come to terms with his deafness, the author gradually evolved a workable philosophy for his life, which he presents in this book in hope it may help other disabled people. Also it gives an insight into how the deaf feel and think, which may help lucky people with full hearing to understand and appreciate the problems of deafness.

About the author

Born in London in February 1920, attended private preparatory school in Gerrards Cross 1927-1933, and Merchant Taylors 1933-1938 where he gained Matriculation exemption and entered Middlesex Hospital in October 1938 as a medical student, leaving in June 1940. After a spell in farming (1940-53) he formed a Churchyard Maintenance service, which is still going strong. Married in 1944, he has two sons and a daughter and lives with his wife near Folkestone.

Author's Note

Some of the material in this book is based on articles written for the RNID magazine *Hearing* over the past twenty years. Some parts seem somewhat dated; I hope this will not cause too much irritation!

My thanks are due to the former editor of *Hearing*, Roy Cole, who did all the preliminary spade work cutting up the articles and arranging them in order, which gave me a starting point. To Anthony Burton-Brown the present editor, whose encouragement was an essential factor.

Finally, I am deeply grateful to Archbishop Donald Coggan who found time in his busy retirement to read the manuscript and write the kind words of commendation.

Michael Jack

Contents

List of Illustrations

Foreword

There are many reasons why I should accede to Michael Jack's request to write a *Foreword* to this little book.

First, he is a good friend of mine. We went to the same school (though I was there long before he was) and underwent similar experiences.

Secondly, I have a hate of untidy churchyards, and he has given well over a quarter of a century to the task of keeping them tidy and making them beautiful — and that, for the most part, within the diocese of which, till recently, I was Archbishop.

Thirdly, he has a sense of humour, and I have found myself chuckling many a time as I read his typescript.

Fourthly, he has something of real wisdom, cheer, and practical help to say to those who themselves have the tremendous handicap of total or partial deafness.

No wonder, then, that I have pleasure in commending these chapters to what I hope will be a wide circle of readers. I wish the book great success.

Sissinghurst
Kent   *The Rt. Rev. The Lord Coggan, D.D.*

Early Days

The snag about being born is that if you don't make a proper job of it, the consequences could be tiresome. It seems (although I have no personal recollection of the fact) that I tried to enter the world by sticking out a cautious toe, upside down; by the time the gynaecologist had twiddled me round and hauled me out I had lost the oxygen from my mother's blood supply before drawing the first breath. One of the first things to suffer from oxygen-lack is the organ of hearing — an impairment of the nervous system and not of the mechanical function which is unaffected.

The precise manner in which my hearing was damaged is dealt with later on. Looking back on my childhood days I cannot remember being deaf; it was when schooling started at the age of seven that I can remember having any difficulty with following the classes. However, in a small school there was never any real trouble, allowances were always made for me. In fact I was top of the class scholastically and also in the cricket and football teams.

The deaf are always victims of the inferiority complex and entering Merchant Taylors School at the age of thirteen laid the foundation for a real king-sized complex which is still liable to operate nearly fifty years later.

I do not remember ever meeting anyone of my own generation who was deaf and I never met anyone who wore a hearing aid — or even had an ear trumpet! In my deafness I was entirely alone, left to battle with it as best I could. My dear school mates never lost an opportunity of making me look a fool, either from my lack of hearing or a slight disclarity in speech. The school in general considered me to be slightly mad, masters as well as boys. My parents bought me a hearing aid with a large battery, a head phone and a microphone with no volume control. It might have been of some use but any attempt at wearing it was met with ridicule from my class mates and even my form master couldn't resist being funny: "Well Jack, where's your telephone today?"

There were slight advantages in being deaf. Games were compulsory but I simply refused to turn up for any rugger matches. Two teams formed from us new boys were taken on a pitch and given instruction in how to play, none of which I followed. The prefect in charge of us suddenly threw the ball to me and when I gazed blankly at it yelled: "RUN, you wretched little sod!!" and gave me a violent push. Obediently I trotted off with the ball, whereupon what seemed like fifty bodies threw themselves on top of me and executed mayhem on my little person. It was, I considered, an extremely rough game and better avoided. My name constantly went down on the playing lists but I never turned up despite wiggings from the games master and eventually they left me alone, evidently considering that as I was deaf and obviously a little mad, it might be better not to push me too hard in case my brains — such as they were — slipped a few more cogs and sent me completely round the bend.

I scored a notable triumph, however, when I was pressganged at the age of fifteen into the Officers' Training Corps. This was an army organisation which every boy was compelled to join unless his parents were pacifists (pretty deadly in a public school), he possessed a heart liable to hand in its cards at the slightest exertion or he had weak legs or something. My parents were not pacifists, my heart was sound and there was nothing wrong with my legs, apart from an uncanny resemblance to those of a female spider.

Therefore I was duly inducted into the O.T.C. and sent square-bashing along with 39 other public school types (which I never was at heart). Determined to oil out of this nasty predicament at all costs, I decided to play up my deafness as never before.

My chance came in the general drilling. The sergeant major shouted his orders from afar; it was genuinely difficult to understand his commands, especially when given from behind our backs. The finest effect came whenever we ordered arms. This involved bringing down the heavy steel-shod muskets beside our feet with a ringing crash. The drill sergeant had the idea that all forty muskets should crash down like one musket... but they never did — not when I was drilling anyway! Like a little Sir Echo, my musket crashed down all on its own, a split second after the others, taking its cue from my neighbour. Thus exhibiting a perfect example of how a deaf cadet could spoil the drill. There were some other little dodges and it took a fortnight or so to perfect the routine but finally it paid off. Going into the armoury one day I was accosted by the major who, looked sorrowfully at me, massaged my arm and said: "Jack — I'm sorry my boy but you are no longer a soldier". I tried to look as if my hopes of rising to be a field marshal had been dashed to the ground but in fact I was so delighted I could have kissed him on both cheeks — which in those days would have had me expelled the following morning. Possibly things have changed nowadays...

It was a trifle embarrassing when I was caught with a duplicate key to the organ as well as with another key which opened most doors in the school — it all took a lot of explaining but there again, my deafness saved me from any punishment. The most awful moment of all was when I arrived in a new classroom a few minutes late and had to sit at the back of the class. In the usual way of masters the world over, Dicky Richards spotted me sneaking in and called out: "Hey, you at the back! What's your name?" I had not the foggiest idea what he was asking me and therefore (as I thought) played safe. "Hum.. That's a difficult question Sir. I'm afraid I have not the slightest idea". The howls of prolonged laughter from the class merely infuriated him. He thought I was trying to be funny and asked a number of chemistry questions — none of which I heard. "How do you make oxygen?" "Well Sir, I usually take our dog for a walk". Finally Dicky could stand it no longer. "Are you DEAF?" he bawled. My quiet "Yes Sir" took the wind out of his sails and he left me alone.

But of course the story went round the school and added to my reputation of being a trifle queer.

From Merchant Taylors School I progressed to the Middlesex Hospital Medical School. My father was a well-known dental surgeon consultant in Queen Anne Street and it was intended that I should follow in his practice. Now my deafness really began to trouble me. The first year, gaining the First M.B. would have been all right had I not fallen deeply in love with my mother's German au pair girl and my brains, being full of Gretel, had little room left for the humdrum business of passing my examinations. I failed and had to retake them as the war began. The second year, starting anatomy and physiology, with its demonstrators around the classes, depressed me very much. It was very difficult to follow what was said, although I do remember clearly the anatomy teacher, Professor Kirk, telling us that the previous year's class had been in the habit of standing their beer bottles on the corpses while dissection was in progress. This, he told us sternly, accompanied by a nasty Scotch glare, would not be tolerated. I gradually drifted away, visiting churches and museums, playing organs whenever opportunity offered itself — Marylebone parish church was my finest clandestine effort.

I used to keep a skeleton under my bed in a cardboard box and once, after a class, took the skull to a dancing class in Baker Street, leaving it on the hall table while I tried to learn the tango. The instructress took great exception to the skull and the girls coming in to dance received such shocks that several of them had to go home immediately. So did I — and anyway found I danced much better by not knowing any steps at all.

It looked as if the time was coming for me and the Middlesex Hospital to part company before the Dean heaved me out. (As P.G. Wodehouse might have written: "Porter! Kindly throw Mr. Jack out — and see that he lands on something sharp").

I told my mother about my plans one morning before she was up that perhaps I had better take up farming. "My God, my only son a farmer!" she moaned and literally turned her face to the wall. I stood on one leg and gave a nervous cough or two before pushing off. There seemed nothing else to do.

Medical students were exempt from being called up for the war and as soon as I left the Middlesex, my call-up papers arrived. At the medical check-up every stitch of clothing had to be removed and I was prodded and examined by a bevy of doctors, each specialising in one aspect of frail humanity. Finally I arrived in front of the ENT man. "Deaf, eh?" he said nastily. "Who is your ENT man?" I told him it was Mr. Wilson of Devonshire Street. The doctor beamed at me: "Why, he is an old friend of mine — well, of course I shall put you down as Grade IV which means you won't be called up".

The Farming Venture

A farmer in Aylesbury was recommended by a patient of my father's and so a pupilship was arranged. It meant living in the farmhouse and acting as a general dogsbody on the farm with the accent on hand milking. The farm was large and the staff were real old timers but a land girl had arrived a few months before me — a former London Hospital nurse. I was much attracted by her pretty appearance and clear voice. I married her three years later and for over thirty-six years have benefited by the clear voice although now, alas, with increasing age my hearing — such as it was — is fading.

I remember one night the herd bull had been separated from the milkers and when I opened the gate at milking time in the winter gloom, calling CUP CUP CUP CUP!!! I suddenly realised that the bull had his head down and was charging straight for me! Moving almost at the speed of light I negotiated a ten strand wire fence running alongside the railway — so fast that to this day I don't know whether I jumped the fence or somehow passed through it in disembodied form, reassembling when safe behind the barrier. Nothing like a charging bull to test one's reflexes.

Milking by hand was always a bore. Some cows were easy and others could be dreadfully hard work. A few were kickers who had to have their hind legs strapped together. A cow kicks sideways and backward, never forward and if you thought your cow was going to kick you shot out your left hand past the near back leg and grabbed hold of its opposite number. This usually saved the milk bucket — not always — and I recall one rotten brute kicking out at the bucket, putting her foot in it, kicking it across the cow shed, landing a third kick on my stool, knocking me over and finally standing triumphantly on my stomach. All done in about five seconds flat. The old hands thought this sort of thing very amusing as they could milk any cow, however tough. Once, after enormous trouble, I had gained a gallon of milk from one young cow and Bert came by, glanced in my pail and said: 'Garn! You ain't milked her". He sat down and expertly removed another gallon. 'Gah!" came his unkind comment, "You couldn't milk a bloody sack".

After two years with this farmer I found myself a job the other side of Aylesbury in Rowsham, on the Leighton Buzzard road. The young

5

farmer, learning that I intended getting married, gave me the tenancy of a farm cottage. We moved in after our honeymoon in April 1944 and it cost three shillings (15p) a week for rent, with free milk, a large garden, a still larger allotment and a hundredweight of potatoes planted with the farmer's which produced half a ton for the winter. My wages were between three and four pounds weekly. We kept laying fowls and later on some pigs and a hive of bees.

In February 1947 we started on our own, renting a farm in Appledore, Kent. From the very beginning the livestock displayed an alarming predilection for premature dying. There was a supposedly in-pig sow we called Massiva but no offspring ever arrived... We utilised the services of a local boar and in due course a litter of piglets arrived. My brother-in-law Philip had joined up with us and a few days later he showed me a small piece of pink skin — all that was left of the litter. Massiva had taken a dislike to her progeny and eaten the lot, overlooking this one piece.

There was a fine fattening pig who was moved into a clean sty, where it immediately staged a heart attack and was dead in ten minutes. Pig meat must be bled if it is to be fit for human consumption so this piggie had to be buried and it took an enormous hole to accommodate it.

On the first Christmas my parents were staying with us. The milking was finished and while I attended to the dairy and cows, Philip got on with feeding the pigs and poultry. He took with him a bucket of oats for the cart horse. This was a dear old mare called Kitty; she was given her Christmas oats and Philip went on his way. Almost immediately he heard a thud, turned round, and there was poor Kitty, flat on the ground, obviously in trouble. He rushed to fetch me but there was nothing to be done. I could only cradle her head in my arms and she died in a few minutes...

I went back to the farm house and took morning tea up to my parents. "Happy Christmas", I called dismally. "The old horse has just dropped down dead".

I do not remember ever seeing two people wake up so quickly. Not only were we very fond of Kitty but only the previous week I had put her in an auction sale with a reserve of fifty pounds on her. The auctioneer, unknown to me, worked in guineas (my hearing had probably let me down again); although Kitty fetched fifty pounds, it was less than fifty guineas and she came home again. We had no use for a horse and sentiment does not usually produce an income.

A book could be written about our adventures during the next six years. Looking back on this episode, I now realise that it was a necessary part of my development. It was a great deal of hard work resulting in an overdraft increasing by five hundred pounds a year. Eventually in 1953 it became obvious that we would have to give up the tenancy. By that time my father had retired from his West End practice and was farming in the next village of Woodchurch and we went to live with him there.

In hindsight, sadder and wiser, I can see Appledore was never a viable venture; the farm was too large for one man but not large enough or intensive enough for two. And perhaps I wasn't a very good farmer... However, if times were sometimes grim and the future looked black, there were some hilarious moments.

We took over with the farm a wartime Fordson tractor — one of the chief aids in winning the battle for food. It had wheels fitted with spade-lugs and in order to travel on the roads we fitted iron bands round the lugs, like gigantic hoops weighing a hundredweight or so. As time went on these tended to wear away and one morning, Philip and I were driving down Appledore's main street when one of the road bands broke loose and bowled smartly ahead of the tractor, making a bee-line for the telephone kiosk. The vicar happened to be passing by and his trained classical mind grasped the situation in a trice. Trotting alongside the hoop, he gave pushes to try and throw it off balance but being a frail old gentleman his pats were quite ineffectual. Philip jumped off the tractor and ran like a maniac down the street and managed to turn the hoop only a few feet before it crashed into the telephone box.

On another occasion, he was not so clever. It was that hard winter of 1947; our outlying fields on Romney Marsh were frozen over and covered thickly with snow. Driving the tractor, Philip guided it on to a patch of hidden ice which immediately gave way, letting down the front wheels into 18 inches of freezing water, he then stalled the engine! For some forgotten reason it was decided I should re-start the tractor, which meant taking off my boots and socks, rolling up my trousers and wading into the freezing water to stand on the ice. I fairly howled at the perfectly extraordinary coldness of the water, but standing on the ice I cranked the engine which fired at about the tenth turn. Philip slowly backed on to firm ground, leaving me to crawl out, legs liberally covered in pale mauve patches.

Among other items taken over with the farm was a saw bench together with an ancient stationary engine to drive it. An examination proved that it was designed to work on a mixture of petrol and water, an apparent lunacy which has seriously come back into the news. Our nerve quite failed us and we tried it on neat petrol; there were no instructions to tell us the proportions of petrol and water. Perhaps when fully warmed up the engine would have run on pure water but as it didn't really run on pure petrol either, we never pursued the matter any further. The circular saw had tiny badly worn teeth, a fact for which I had cause to be grateful later on, when they managed only to gnaw off half my forefinger instead of removing it in one fell swoop.

Having examined the engine and primed it with the three necessary ingredients, I fitted the starting handle and gave a few pulls. Absolutely nothing happened. Philip spat on his hands, seized the handle and twirled it with such savage ferocity that the engine was compelled to burst into life, which it did so suddenly that it caught him unawares. The crank handle was snatched out of his hands and sent whirling round and round. We backed away hastily and just as well, for a moment later the handle flew off and went clean through the tin roof. I rushed forward with a small log and pushed it against the saw. The whole caboodle stopped immediately! The ancient engine was frightfully temperamental and several times the starting handle was chucked at our heads and only some nifty footwork saved us. There was hardly enough power to cut through anything thicker than a rotten old bean pole. We gave it up as hopeless and I bought a pulley take-off gear for the tractor.

A Shorthorn bull was included in the farm livestock. He was supposed to be a pedigree bull although we never saw any document to that effect; it was just one of those things rumoured around the village. Down on Romney Marsh by the Military Canal I had some acres of grazing for some of the cattle and Willie Moo-Moo (as small son Nicholas called him) was taken down to run with them. It was not long before the neighbouring farmer 'phoned up to say that Willie had swum a dyke and joined his herd of pedigree Ayreshires.

On Romney Marsh dykes filled with water are often used instead of fencing. We therefore went down after breakfast the next day to bring Willie back to the farm buildings. This, in theory, merely meant opening a few gates to admit him to the main road along which we would drive him back to the farm. We got him through the gates all right but then he would keep swimming back across the dykes, leaving us to toil round to the gates and start all over again. One thing, however, he was quite the gentleman and waited politely for us to catch up with him... Eventually we did manage to trick him on to the road and got him back as far as the pumping station. He spied the five-barred gate leading to the canal bank, jumped it at a bound and trotted off back to his forbidden ladies, from whom he had parted three hours earlier! He possessed a fine sense of topography, did Willie-Moo-Moo.

After lunch we tried again, taking with us an old farm worker who even in June was muffled up to the eyebrows like all old farm workers. Portions of his garments were removed at intervals as we ran about the Marsh under the hot sun until at the finish the old chap was trotting about in hardly more than his underpants. It was said in his village that this old labourer had bitten off his father's ear in the course of an argument and had promptly spat it out on the kitchen range and allowed it to frizzle merrily... Oh yes, we did eventually get Willie back into his pen but it took five of us.

Our 'daily' who did the house hardly came into the category 'old farm workers' and she certainly didn't overdress. One balmy summer dawn she was discovered blissfully asleep in a ditch with her sister, both stark naked, each with a pound note stuck to her midrib with chewing gum. There were lots of American soldiers about in those days. Not that she was narrow minded about nationality. She kept a pet German p.o.w. hidden in her woodshed for quite a time.

A great many other perfectly extraordinary things happened happened in those six years such as the Drunken Cow.

I had sold the dairy herd in one fell swoop — another story perhaps — and retained one cow for the house milk. This cow, Stewart, was a bit queer, like most of our livestock and one night she broke into the orchard and stuffed herself to bursting point with rotting windfall apples. I found her in the morning, brought her into the loose-box to milk her, when she at once laid herself down and quietly went to sleep. Highly perturbed, I phoned up our vet who came out, examined her (still in deep slumber) and then he laughed heartily. "Your damn cow is as drunk as a lord", he shouted. "She'll be okay in a day or so and then have a terrible hangover".

Well, that was all right, but how about milking her? There she lay, flat out on the loose-box straw smiling gently to herself and possibly dreaming of a white Christmas. I had an idea, trotted up to our local garage and borrowed the endless chain tackle which the mechanic used to hoist engines out of cars. With one end fastened to an overhead beam and the other to a stout strap round Stewart's waist, I had only to haul on the chain and up she rose. Very limp she was too and looked more like a pantomime cow than the real thing but at least she could be milked. Only it was not milk which came out but pure cream. The cider inside her (sorry!) seemed to have started up a personal internal cream separator and squeezing it out of her was the hardest milking I'd ever done in 12 years of farming!

I sold Stewart to a dealer when the time came for us to leave. He came along with a halter which he tied round her neck and by which he proposed leading her to pastures new. I warned him that she was an unusual sort of cow (even her name) but he wouldn't listen. "There ain't nothing I don't understand about cows", he said as he went off, pulling Stewart behind him. His mixed bag of negatives could be read either way. By the time he'd reached the top of the lane, Stewart had taken charge (as I could have told him from years of experience with her) and the last we saw of the pair of them was a small cloud of dust moving rapidly into the wilds of Romney Marsh. Whether he really meant to go that way I have no idea. We never saw him again and in fact heard long afterward that he had committed suicide.

Then there was the time I knocked over a bee hive with a motor mower and had to flee into the farmhouse pursued by a cloud of angry bees. I got through the door first and not only locked it but bolted it top and bottom for good measure, feeling pretty sure that even *my* bees would not be equal to breaking down a door.

We took with us down to Kent an elderly Baby Austin, 1931 vintage, which we called Leonard, after Leonard Rabbidge in The Fast Lady. Later we bought a Flying Standard Nine and decided to turn Leonard into a utility vehicle. Philip and I did this by standing on opposite sides of Leonard, each with a hacksaw and cutting off the roof and sides behind the front seats. We mounted a wooden platform supported by two angle irons lashed to the back axle and Leonard went all over the farm, picking up boxes of fruit and vegetables, carting out farmyard manure and running errands around the neighbourhood. He even went to Hastings, eighteen miles away, loaded with runner beans and peas. He couldn't negotiate Guestling Hill in bottom gear and went up it backward!

The author sitting in Leonard, about 1951. Two 'harvest campers' standing by the side. Inset: Haymaking with Leonard.

"Let the organ thunder!" Author in Canterbury Cathedral

Lord and Lady Coggan with the author, his wife and daughter.

Photo taken by Piers Plowright when the BBC interviewed me for a radio programme on modern attitudes to death.

Thinking it over, Leonard now seems quite incredible — not only my nerve in driving this erratic old vehicle round the countryside but actually getting away with it police-wise. One cop who saw me unloading beans at Appledore station suggested that if Leonard ventured into Ashford I'd be hanged. Once a steering pin dropped out and we veered into the ditch and I had to walk home. It created a sensation in the village as everyone thought that mad young Mr. Jack had done himself in at last... Bitter was their disappointment to see me later in the day still driving Leonard. We pulled him out with the farm tractor and put the pin back.

The inevitable happened... The police, who had been pretty tolerant after the war, began to crack down on motoring offences. Although he was still taxed and insured, Leonard was really a motoring offence in himself and no longer went on the roads. But I ran out of paraffin ploughing down the road, walked home, loaded some fuel on to Leonard and chugged off back to the field. Jangling along at twenty miles an hour, I spied a motor cycle cop coming towards me. "This is it", I muttered to myself, having gained the field and seen him heading back towards me.

To cut a painful story short, a traffic inspector came out and examined Leonard in the field. He went a dirty white colour as he checked him over and said it was the worst case he'd ever encountered. There followed a summons, of course, and the charges took up most of the sheet. Everything wrong with Leonard (and there was a great deal) was carefully tabulated. Inefficient brakes, inefficient steering (and the steering column waved about in graceful fashion), no front lights, no rear lights, no tax disc on display, a missing number plate, front wheels wobble and no windscreen wipers were some of the items. (Since there was no windscreen anyway, there seemed no call for wipers). I did tell the cop when he first stopped me that the headlights were so bright I had to remove the bulbs but this did not amuse him very much. He took his work very seriously. In all there were nine charges. The RAC lawyer who came to defend me suggested we show the magistrates a photograph of Leonard and get a good laugh which might earn me a donation from public funds for cheering up the court. I produced a photograph and he was perfectly aghast — he couldn't possibly show THAT to the magistrates! When the case came up he treated it in a light-hearted manner and after careful deliberation the bench fined me ten shillings each for the brakes and steering and half-a-crown each on the other seven charges — a total of thirty-seven and sixpence!! The photograph was given to the traffic inspector who certified Leonard as unroadworthy and he was delighted with his gift.

My eldest son, Nicholas, then five, was always pestering me to let him drive Leonard and finally I gave in. He let in the clutch with a jerk, put the accelerator pedal down to the floor board and we roared down the farm lane in bottom gear bumping and lurching from side to side. There was a fleeting glimpse of the pigs' amazed white faces as we hurtled past their sties, cows bellowed, hens flapped. Nicholas drove clean (?) through a heap of steaming pig manure and crashed against the vicarage fence; the shock threw the battery into the radiator. No real damage done apart from a bent starting handle!

Organs and Churches

I always loved music and had taken up the piano at an early age; had continued at Merchant Taylors but as I never practised, finding my music teacher wholly uninterested in my progress besides giving me monumentally dull pieces to learn, my father refused to pay for further lessons — and who could blame him? I carried on playing for my own pleasure; like many musicians I had visions of becoming a conductor but any idea of being a budding Henry Wood were knocked on the head when I found I could happily 'conduct' a Mozart symphony under the impression it was a Rossini overture.

The organ had always interested me, although hearing little of its full variety and beauty, and it seemed a good idea to persevere with it. The church organ with all its stops out could be depended upon to drown out any opposition from choirs, congregations or rival instruments. If I chose to play Mozart on that, anyone trying to play Rossini would speedily have to change his tune.

So deafness or no deafness, with the organ I have persevered, once as a full-time village organist cassocked and surpliced, or as an occasional deputy.

But some hearing and a thoroughly reliable hearing aid are essential. It is not possible to accompany a church service unless one can hear the singing and the officiating minister. I speak from painful experience.

I had still no hearing aid, managing to get by with my unaided hearing. However, using the tractor without a silencer for two days induced a set of virulent and useless head noises. (Useless in the sense that they could not be sold, put to work or otherwise made to earn their keep). So I went back to my Devonshire Street ENT man after an absence of many years and he told me to go to a certain hospital where I would be issued with the new *absolutely free* hearing aid and batteries on the National Health Service. Overjoyed at the thought of at last getting something for nothing I trotted off to the hospital and was issued without delay with one of the original Medresco aids, together with a few vague hints on its use. Only later did I discover that there was a tremendous queue waiting for the Medresco aids. Knowing the right man had shot me to the top!

That first Medresco was a perfect nuisance, if that does not seem ungrateful. It had two batteries strapped in their leather case round my waist or bulging in my pocket. An active farmer, I found the package very irksome while the ear cord was an absolute menace, getting caught up in everything from apple trees to chicken feathers and cows' tails. I never wore it while working and not very often at other times which was probably as well or it might have gone the way of my watch when I was kicked by a cow while milking her and a flying hoof sliced it neatly off my wrist and it ended up in a pail of milk.

I was twelve when I first started playing the organ and from then until 1948 I played for pleasure; at Merchant Taylors School I had sung bass in the boarding house choir. In 1948, after a year on our own farm, the vicar kindly allowed me to play the parish church organ whenever I liked. At Easter I joined the church choir and the following week the organist handed in his resignation and went off to Norfolk. This, so it was carefully explained, was pure coincidence.

The vicar was at his wits' end to find someone willing to become village organist and eventually he turned up at the farm and asked if I'd mind playing occasionally for the evening services. Reflecting quickly on the fact that the evening congregation was almost non-existent, it would not matter much if I made a mess of the service — as seemed most likely. I heartily told him he could rely on me to help out. Being unable, in the next two days, to find anyone willing to play at all, he first returned to ask if I'd play every Sunday evening and then to take on the full job as village organist. I sagged more than somewhat at his last remark, my knees went all weak at the corners and had I not taken a generous swig of the thick syrup being taken to feed the bees, I should have fallen flat on the ground.

One might confidently have asserted that the vicar, faced with an inexperienced and deafish organist, would choose a very simple service. Not a bit of it! He laid on his usual second-Sunday-of-the-month service which began with Matins and then suddenly leaped headlong into the Communion service, beginning with the Ten Commandments. Doubtless he thought that as there was bound to be a muddle somewhere, an extra good one would make little difference. I spent most of my time before the Sunday with terrible stomach pains — a beastly mixture of butterflies and flat-irons having a free-for-all in my tum.

By Sunday morning I was an absolute bag of nerves, hardly able to stand and quite unable to follow anything said to me. The actual organ-playing presented no difficulty; apart from the usual 'nerves' there was the uncertainty of hearing the service. At five to eleven, feeling like someone about to make his first parachute jump, I moved on to the organ stool and began to grind out some kind of voluntary; the vicar and choir duly processed in.

All went well until the Te Deum; the place was lost almost immediately and I staggered alone from line to line with absolutely no idea of where I was, nor even, indeed, where the church was. Eventually I stopped playing. There was a dead silence in church. Everyone watched with intense excitement to see if the new organist was going to throw an epileptic fit. Turning round to one of the choirmen I demanded hoarsely: "Where the deuce are we?" to which he hissed back: "The noble army of Martyrs" — which summed it up very well. This mistake never happened again; there were a number of occasions when the place was lost but luckily regained before chaos set in.

Provided the words were in view it was easy enough to follow parson or choir but if the place was lost or they were strange words not in my book then I found it impossible to distinguish any sense at all. If, therefore, the vicar put in a new prayer, I could never be sure when he had reached the end which was my cue to play Amen. On a number of occasions I gave him an Amen when he wasn't ready for it — he simply carried on with his prayer thus obliging me to try again.

Same with the lessons — I never heard a word all the seven years as village organist. One reader in particular sounded like a senile oboe — I didn't have the foggiest notion what he was reading. If he paused overlong I immediately leaped in with the next chant. Should the pause be merely due to a frog in the throat or two bible pages stuck together, a choirman would reach round and give my surplice a sharp tug, upon which I immediately knocked off playing and tried again a few minutes later. Our M.P. once came to evensong and the Magnificat chant was played over three times — surely some sort of record? It would have been nice to push a button and send the whole miserable outfit — the organ and its wretched player — whirling away into the basement in happy oblivion! But that only happened in the Super Cinemas.

The vicar was a very absent-minded old man and he could never remember to warn me of any service changes. On my part I couldn't hear him give them out in church; in any case I was absent-minded myself and quite likely to forget. He once inducted a Roman Catholic into the C. of E. and used some of the communion service. Besides being deaf I thought I was going mad — trying to figure out what was happening.

It was never any use anyone coming up and whispering instructions during a service; they were inaudible. Sometimes notes were written — if there was a pencil with a point to hand which had not already rolled away under the organ pedal keyboard.

Eventually I moved to another village and played the organ when wanted. Wearing a hearing aid became essential since the organ was so far from the rector it was impossible to catch my cues. It made me wish I had used my Medresco much earlier in Appledore days; a great gain to one's peace of mind to follow clearly every word.

Mistakes in services were not always my fault. One Sunday I deputised in a neighbouring church and the vicar explained that on that particular Sunday he had the Litany and to avoid an over-long service he cut out the Venite. "I see, Vicar. After the Lord's Prayer and Responses you will announce the psalm?" "That's it, Mr. Jack" the old cleric beamed, "After the Lord's Name be Praised I will give out the psalm". And what actually happened? The old ass clean forgot it was Litany Sunday and awaited my play-over of the Venite chant! "No Venite — Litany Sunday!" I hissed at him. He stared blankly. A choir lady went over and whispered in his ear. He continued to look as though he was sitting on a plate of hot porridge. Finally deciding that his organist's brains must have slipped a few cogs, he announced that the Venite would be "said'. It was, too, and I felt a complete fool but the sharpest hearing in the world would have done me no good on that occasion.

The thing which gave the most trouble was the saying of the Banns. The vicar hardly ever remembered to tell me when he had Banns to announce and if he did I either didn't hear or immediately forgot all about it. He would rise to his feet after the second lesson and begin his patter which I generally missed through being fully occupied in playing over the next chant. A tug on my surplice and I would politely give the vicar a chance to say his piece. Once he had two sets of Banns and I played over the chant three times — a record unequalled since the time of James II.

I refused to wear the Medresco for Sunday organ playing since not only did it make the organ sound totally different but I couldn't be bothered to hang all the bits and pieces under my cassock. I just muddled along for seven years; Amens in the middle of prayers and chants thrown out halfway through the lessons became normal routine accepted as part of the service, like the old vicar's dog. Occasionally he turned up in church during a service, looking for his master, and thereby caused some odd interjections. ("Our Father, which art in Heaven — down Druid! — Hallowed be Thy Name — Druid, go away! —" and so on).

In 1955 my mother presented me with a pair of hearing-aid spectacles which were marvellous. Better reproduction than the Medresco and naturally placed hearing — at my ear instead of from inside my waistcoat pocket. However the earpieces were thick and heavy, causing the tips of my ears to assume a fairly horizontal appearance. This aid eventually turned queer and was posted back to the company who had told me they operated a three-day postal repair service. It was retained for three weeks and sent back with the frame so bent I could have worn it only had my eyes been in the position as portrayed by Charles Laughton in the Hunchback of Notre Dame — one eye two inches higher than the other. The aid was returned to the firm who retained it for another three weeks, finally sending it back in working wearing order but calling it 'obsolete' and offering to sell me their latest model.

Churchyard Consultant

In 1953 it became obvious that the farm venture was a failure. The landlord would only sell the farm to us at an inflated price and we could not afford to carry on. The question was — what were we to do? By then we had two boys aged six and eight and a baby was on the way. We would have no home, I had no training in any other business, we had heavy debts...

At that time a new vicar took over the parish. He had asked me to tidy up the overgrown churchyard — which was only cut by the churchwarden when he wanted some hay for his rabbits. Having some grass-cutting machinery on the farm I made a good job of the churchyard and then the vicar (who knew what was happening to us) made his momentous suggestion. Why not offer a churchyard maintenance service? At the same time my father, who had retired from his West End practice, took a farm in nearby Woodchurch and offered us a home. That was one problem solved.

Acting on the vicar's suggestion I sent out ninety copies of a circular letter to all clergy within a thirty mile range, offering to set up a churchyard maintenance service if the demand made it worthwhile. The telephone began ringing the following morning and fifteen of my letters were answered. Yes, please come and help us with our churchyard problems, was the universal plea! So in August 1953 I started a churchyarding service which is still going strong twenty-eight years later without the need for further advertising.

There are a number of questions everyone asks me and here are the answers to the more obvious ones. I use a 10/12 cwt Ford Transit van to carry the machinery around. It will hold anything up to five mowers — which I may need on a local lawn mowing round. For the churchyard work it carries a 6 H.P. rotary mower and a couple of smaller hand rotary mowers or if the work involves cutting stuff up to seven feet high the old-type Allen Motor Scythe is put aboard. Churchyards mown every two or three weeks require rough-cut lawn mowers. There are also many other permanent items in the van such as shears, loppers, secateurs, a few spare parts, various types of weedkilling sprays and a good range of tools, nuts and bolts, washers and so forth for overhauls and adjustments. For twenty-six years the vans also conveyed my two Dog-Mates, first an Australian Terrier called Beetle and then for fourteen years my small Griffon Nobby. They were both great characters, especially Nobby, who learned to read (although very slowly) and when not working in churchyards he sat in the van and read books, mostly by Dornford Yates. He had another odd trait — he would prefer drinking water straight from the tap; he knew where all the churchyard taps were and would wait underneath them for someone to turn on a trickle of water.

The average weekly mileage travelled in the grass cutting season would be between two and three hundred miles. The longest journey is 35 miles and the shortest a few hundred yards. For most of these years I have maintained over forty churchyards almost single-handed; my wife usually helps me to mow Wye churchyard (near Ashford) fortnightly.

This sounds a staggering total but it must be remembered I do not work at trade union speeds and it is possible to mow four or even five smaller churchyards in a day. The work must be planned carefully in advance to accomplish the maximum work with the minimum mileage.

For the first five years I used only a rough grass cutter, the Allen Scythe, each churchyard having two or three cuts a season. It meant cutting them one week and clearing the hay the following Saturday when my family and friends came out with me as paid helpers. We thought nothing of igniting twenty bonfires in the course of the day. In 1958 I started using large rotary mowers, the grass was chewed up and left to rot so the time saved was used to give extra cuts — generally five or six during the season. Over the years during the winter I have levelled off all my churchyards, removing mounds, curbs, footstones, body stones and occasional bumble vaults.

Churchyards can therefore be divided into three categories. Most are rotary mown, a very few with difficult areas still have a rough-cut twice a season with hay clearance while places with more cash to spare have a fortnightly or three-weekly mowing with rough-cut lawn mowers which produce an excellent finish, the grass being allowed to rot away where it lies — and even after twenty-five years of this treatment my cemeteries and churchyard lawns show no traces of the grass that has been left behind all those years.

We moved to Hythe in 1958 and a year later I was asked to take on some local lawns for elderly people no longer able to do their own mowing. The first year there were six, at present it is over forty-five, none of which I asked for or sought. It would be easy to double or treble this, such is the demand but I say *no* more often than *yes* since churchyards are my main interest. But as retirement age begins to loom nearer, the obvious thing to do is to cut down on the harder churchyard work and take on more mowing. All these lawns are within a quarter of an hour of my home so the time saved in driving around Kent and into Sussex is considerable.

"Ah", say the pundits, "but what do you do in the winter?" For the first twenty-four years from January to March I was levelling churchyards to fit them for rotary mowing. This job has dried up (I never advertised the service) and in its place has come a lot of small estate work in Hythe, with some private gardening, tree felling, generally tidying up places for which there was no time in the summer.

In the early spring the churchyard round begins again, not grass cutting but spraying round gravestone and church walls to keep down weeds, reducing the amount of time spent on hand trimming in the busy months. Probably a few tree branches need attention after winter gales. The actual mowing begins around Easter and carries on until Christmas Eve. Holidays therefore have to be taken out of season — often more preferable but the weather can be colder and the days shorter.

This lawn mowing business is something which any deaf person ought to consider as a way of making a living. I soon discovered that for a deafish man, self-employment is the only way in which real satisfaction and peace of mind can come.

Employers may be kind, workmates tolerant, but all too often not. The fear of 'the sack' hangs more heavily over the deafie than the hearing — he can be sure of being one of the first redundancies when hard times come. Misunderstanding, exasperation, impatience, surround him when orders cannot be properly heard or warnings heeded. If the deaf charities spent more time and more money teaching young deaf people how to set up on their own instead of trying to compete at the factory gates or the office desk, there would be more happiness all round.

1953 was indeed the turning point in my life, when contentment, happiness and hard work all arrived together because I had found this way of earning a tolerable and healthy open air living *on my own*. I shall never cease to urge self-employment for the deaf and hard of hearing — some of them anyway — who find difficulty working with people in public places or even individuals. All this time later the theme comes back to me with redoubled force. For I remain convinced

The author investigating a broken vault and getting trapped in the process!

A "ghost" photo of Charmian in Ickham Churchyard

"Nobby" with my wife Audrey and daughter Charmian in Swalecliffe Churchyard some years ago.

Sons Nicholas and Nigel smashing 39 bodystones in 5 hours (Note transistor radio)

24

there are many 'service jobs' which would be suitable for our disability. Offering a service of some kind to the community can be a reward in itself even though the modern way of thought seems to be against this.

My services fulfill a need and I would say that anyone with a mechanical bent, who can work hard, has some idea of business methods and can drive a car, could succeed as well as I have done. In addition to the above qualities I would add further the need to be reliable (which some contractors are not), honest in dealing with the clients (old folk especially are not always too good with money — one lady gave me a fiver instead of a pound note) and also, maybe, to be of cheerful countenance even when one feels the opposite.

This grass-cutting business meets only one aspect of community needs. In my area there is a constant and unsatisfied demand for jobbing gardeners. They need not be experts; just someone willing to tidy up an overgrown border, clip the grass verges; things which an ailing or elderly owner cannot manage. There is scope here for deaf people with no mechanical aptitude whatever; a bicycle or even shank's pony would move them round the work and most householders would have the necessary tools. It doesn't require conversation; written messages or signs would suffice.

Around my home area there is also a chronic shortage of window cleaners. We gave up trying to find one years ago and clean our own. People turn up sometimes but usually they either fail to appear again or charge the earth, frequently both!

There are other chores which need doing — such as odd-jobbing for private people, perhaps too elderly to tackle many jobs or maybe the husband has died and his widow cannot manage jobs such as window cleaning, changing light bulbs, mending fuses, moving furniture around, hanging a sagging gate, replacing a leaking water tap washer — all those other household jobs which keep turning up. The point about these sorts of job is that they are best found through recommendations from satisfied customers.

Elderly women living alone are an easy prey to unscrupulous contractors. Time and time again I have been asked to call at some house and the old lady or gentleman has said: "Mrs. So and So says that you were very helpful and she is sure I can rely on you". If I say that I have no time to spare but that there are people advertising in the local paper, these old folk are usually most reluctant to answer such advertisements, pointing out, rightly, that nothing is known of the contractors concerned. If this is only for lawn mowing, with how much greater force will this apply for jobs within the house itself?

I need hardly elaborate on the theme of how a personal service may be built up. Perhaps a verse from Psalm 15 could be taken as a motto: "He that sweareth unto his neighbour and disappointeth him not, though it were to his own hindrance".

It would probably be necessary to advertise at first to gain some contacts; maybe a firm of estate agents would be glad to have a reliable contractor to attend to the outside maintenance of blocks of flats which they manage — cut the grass, keep flower beds tidy, and do the odd repair jobs which builders never seem to want nowadays. I have four such small estates; the residents know to whom to apply if they need some help and they are very good at spreading the word around their friends.

Nowadays we are lumbered with a lot of bureaucratic paperwork; if your turnover is under £15,000 annually there is no need to operate VAT. Operating a service means there are no large capital sums involved. Unless you have a business brain which ever seeks to expand and make more and more money, I would say, work by yourself. The moment you take on additional labour you are going to be faced with additional problems — not only of hearing but items such as operating pay-as-you-earn, insurance stamps — and also the worry of your workers' output and reliability and heaven knows what else. Keep the business to yourself is a good motto. Remember, many people grow ambitious, expand their little business and sometimes go bankrupt because the wages cannot be met, labour has let the employer down and the end is Queer Street, besides a load of extra worries and maybe an ulcer into the bargain.

Strict book-keeping is necessary for tax purposes and a careful record of the daily work kept in a Boots diary or something similar. I might cut twenty lawns one day and four churchyards the next and if all of it was not booked down on arrival home at night it would be impossible to keep track of progress and send out regular accounts.

If a deafish ass like myself can make a go of his business for more than a quarter of a century, surely anyone else can do likewise — and make more money than I can be bothered to do!

Holidays

One great drawback to the churchyarding business is the holiday problem. At the hottest time of the year one is naturally engaged in working from early morning until late in the evening six days a week. There is little chance of any time off in the busy season which for me extends from the end of April to the end of October. We therefore try and fit in some sort of break either in early spring before the lawn mowing gets under way or in September when there is not the same urgency about lawn mowing. I can recall two particularly good holidays.

"Come and see me some time before I grow too granny-like" wrote Gretel, my pre-war German girl-friend whom I had not met for twenty-eight years.

So my wife and I decided to have a German holiday in September 1967 and take fourteen-year-old daughter Charmian, who was learning German at school and would benefit from hearing it being spoken all round her for eight days.

I doubt if I could have summoned up the courage to face a foreign country on my own. I often have job enough to understand English conversation, let alone French and German, with all the inquiries, comments and so forth that a sea/land journey entails. You cannot keep on saying "Sorry?" But blessed with an excellent practical wife with a strong sense of humour, willing to do the listening if I did the talking, I decided to take the plunge and drive our A35 from Zeebrugge to Solingen (other side of Cologne) a distance of about 230 miles.

The amount of preparation took me aback — booking car ferry, green card car insurance, insurances for medical care, luggage, etc., passports — but all this was paperwork and therefore easily dealt with. A Cordon Bleu from the R.A.C. covered medical attention and mechanical aid for the car, transport by other means should the car pack up completely or be wrecked, and garage vouchers to avoid spending one's own money abroad. In fact, had the unfortunate need arisen, we were covered to the extent of being brought back in our coffins ready screwed down for burial!

The passport photographs I took myself, in the garden; they gained instant dislike. "We don't look as awful as that'. So glum! So peculiar!" "Nonsense — excellent likenesses — and think what I saved by doing it myself".

My ears let me down immediately after boarding the ferry boat at Dover, scheduled to leave at midnight. A voice boomed and crackled from loudspeakers all over the ship. "What did it say?" I nervously demanded of my wife. "Oh nothing for you to worry about", she said cheerfully. "The back of the ship has fallen off or something and we shall be late starting". The public address system gave tongue at intervals during the trip but I never caught a single word — you cannot lip-read a loudspeaker.

We had a cabin and slept for much of the journey, being woken up just before four o'clock as the ship entered Zeebrugge harbour. I went up on deck — it was still dark — to see lights stretching for miles on shore and winking harbour lights all round me. This was the most thrilling moment of the whole trip, literally venturing into the unknown, facing a journey through two countries, driving on the right, strange languages and strange money. I might add that I had been worrying about this right-hand driving for weeks but there was nothing in it; after half-an-hour I ceased to bother.

It proved necessary to take more care at crossings and roundabouts. Thus, turning left in this country you simply turn left and carry on along the new road whereas on the continent you must go right over your new road and then turn left — just as we go to the far side to turn right. Towns with one-way traffic were a worry and in Solingen I scouted round on foot to see how the traffic behaved. I had fitted my headlamps with amber plastic lenses which turned the left-hand dip system to the right. All motorists used dipped headlights even when driving in brightly lit cities. I don't know how I would have managed without the lenses. Without them my dip would have been in the centre of the road, certain to provoke resentment from oncoming drivers.

My wife worried in case the motion of the boat upset her — and a force 9 gale had been predicted for our crossing. The R.A.C. man, when appealed to at the docks, said conditions "weren't too bad", which meant anything or nothing since his idea of a bad crossing might have been quite different from ours.

So to be on the safe side she took two seasickness pills and bitterly regretted it since they made her not only appallingly sleepy but also gave her a painfully dry mouth. It gradually wore off over the next 12 hours. Charmian took one pill. When the time came to drive off the ship and begin our journey they behaved like walking corpses and from a navigation view (helping me with the route, looking out for signs etc) they were as helpful. My wife was practically out on her feet and in consequence I missed a Liege turning on the Brussels by-pass and had to go back through the city and along the ordinary road. We did not pick up the Ostend-Aachen motorway until after Liege, which was our first stop for breakfast. It was fortunate that I had not taken any of this sickness remedy; I would have been quite unfit to drive. This is a point worth remembering.

We arrived in Liege before the shops were open so we parked the car in a small square and Charmian and I scouted around for a breakfast cafe and by the time we had found one and returned to the car, a small agitated attendant had drifted up. For all the use speech was to us we might as well have been stone deaf. My daughter's understanding of French spoken in Belgium was exactly nil. As a matter of fact, whenever I appealed to her for a German or French word it generally turned out that she 'hadn't done it yet'. I have some halting French and German which invariably sent her into fits of semi-hysterical laughter whenever I opened my mouth. But at least the natives often understood me!

Arguing with the attendant and waving our arms about in expansive gestures attracted the notice of a policeman who moved up in a friendly way and joined in the discussion. We had overstepped our parking time but we made him understand we had eaten nothing since leaving England and could we stay 'une autre demie-heure', which he obligingly allowed.

The drive to Cologne was uneventful. The city is encircled by an autobahn on each side; they subsequently meet, one passing under the other with the usual access roads. I drove on to the wrong road and carried on for 25 miles before we realised something was wrong. Once on an autobahn you may be stuck for many miles unable to get off on to the other track or make a U-turn. At a steady 50-55 m.p.h. we were one of the slowest vehicles on the road — there is no speed limit and the Continentals are certainly much faster and harder drivers than the English; very little of the give-the-other-fellow-a-courtesy. Even huge lorries thundered past at 70 m.p.h. pulling large trailers — their wheels reached nearly to our roof level. To show their contempt for the crawling English beetle the lorry drivers passed with only a foot clearance, their slip-streams shaking our small car. I was glad my hearing lessened the pounding and roaring of these enormous vehicles. The autobahns are wonderful though. Extremely fast, beautiful surface, relatively few bends and a marvellous way of getting places quickly. This was 13 years ago and of course we have done our own thing since then.

Our friends took us down to Bonn at a steady 80 or 90 miles an hour. You must, however, know exactly where you are going and which turning off you need to take. Plenty of warning is given in advance of each turning — relatively few and far between — and it is difficult to slow down to a crawl trying to decide whether to turn off or not, since the slow traffic may be travelling anything up to 50, and a 100 m.p.h. in the fast lane. A deaf ditherer could easily cause a nasty pile-up and I noticed the German drivers shook their fists at each other at the slightest provocation.

It is a well-known theory that it is not necessary to speak a foreign language; one has merely to shout loudly and distinctly in English. This was a complete wash-out. No amount of shouting got us anywhere. A few quiet words of German were nearly always understood by everyone but my own family who remained in the background, quivering with mirth. One result of my holiday was merely to confirm that I cannot learn languages by ear. I have to see the words written down to grasp their syllabic content before the pronunciation is understood.

My hearing aid, excellent though it is, proved disappointing in grasping German, though I suspect a longer stay would have worked wonders. I simply could not grasp the spoken word but if written down I could at once translate it. But then, all my life I have pronounced vegetable as 'vegable' and Christopher as 'Chrispofer'; so foreign words are equally liable to go astray. You need a phrase book, some carefully rehearsed basic sentences and a dictionary. Armed thus, you can adapt the phrases to suit the need, supplying words from the dictionary, merely pointing to the word if the pronunciation eludes you.

We were fortunate in staying with two old friends of mine in Solingen, living ten minutes' car journey apart. My daughter Charmian stayed with my friend who spoke excellent English but when we had left her for the night she spoke German only to Charmian. They did not, thank goodness, try it on me — having found that a perfectly useless waste of time before the war!

With my friend, Gretel, we visited Cologne, shopping, and looking round the cathedral. At 5.15 p.m. Gretel suggested we bought some cakes and took them home to eat for tea. At 7.15 p.m. we were still tramping the streets in the dark, looking for our car, which we had left near a large old gateway — remains, I guess, of the old city wall. Gretel confessed she did not know Cologne very well and it turned out there were half a dozen of these old gateways scattered around the city! Finally, growing desperate, she hailed a passing taxi, told him where we had entered the city. The taxi bowled off and we were glad to rest our aching feet. Glancing out of the window I suddenly spied our car. 'Mein auto!!" I screamed. The taxi screeched to a halt. What a feeling of relief — tempered by losing our way immediately trying to gain the autobahn home. Gretel again battled valiantly for us inquiring the way. Had I been forced to do the talking I doubt if we should ever have found the car: our bodies would have been buried by the authorities in some quiet spot...

Both families took us round castles and palaces. I preferred it without a guide since it is difficult enough to follow a guide in this country unless standing close enough to have the assistance of lip-reading; in a foreign country it was hopeless. We were particularly tickled by the very sensible custom of providing enormous felt slippers about eighteen inches long, which are worn over one's walking shoes to protect the highly polished wood or marble floors. A crowd of 50 people sliding about in these felt boats was a very amusing sight!

We found German prices roughly on a par with our own. The Rhine wine was very cheap in those days, from 20p a bottle upwards according to quality; we drank it very often. However, the Germans are very hot on drinking and driving, their legal limits are lower than ours and strictly enforced. I was not allowed to drive my friends home if I had had more than one glass of wine since if I were involved in an accident — even if no fault of mine — I would have been in trouble.

My wife and daughter found it odd to sit in a restaurant and hear the babble of incomprehensible talking going on round them. I told them that this was my experience every day of my life, since, being unable to hear casual conversation, it makes no difference what the language happens to be.

Walking through the park one morning I was delighted to see some motor mowers and hurried over to examine them with a professional eye. There was a smallish stoutish man in charge of them and by suitable signs and gestures I gave him to understand I controlled a fleet of 12 mowers at home. He stared in respectful amazement. "So?"

I pulled up my trouser leg and showed him some scars received from flying rotary mower stones. "Aaah ja!" He pulled up his trouser leg, revealing dark green long pants and bright blue socks. His leg was pitted with scars — an easy winner!

Crossing the streets is carefully regulated. In towns you are supposed to cross at traffic lights and then only when a little green man is showing. When two little red men were illuminated no crossing is allowed even though the road might be empty. The English custom of darting in and out of traffic or waiting until the road lights turn green and then stepping slowly off the pavement would probably result in an on-the-spot fine if a policeman caught you, though an English visitor would probably be merely cautioned, since we are considered to be an eccentric race. In Solingen one morning I crossed with a large crowd, behaving just as they did and turning off along my new pavement. I vaguely heard a shout but took no notice until I realised everyone was staring at me. Looking over my shoulder I saw a policeman (in his green uniform) evidently calling me. What had I done wrong? I flashed him a toothy grin and flapped a large hand in acknowledgement. For all I know he had merely jested: "What a tall Englander!"

One thing I failed to do while on holiday was to browse round some churchyards. I was told I had enough churchyards at home and was on holiday. Still, I managed to escape twice and secured two excellent colour shots of Roman Catholic churchyards — most beautifully kept and chock full of growing plants. I was interested to see that some graves had little lighted candles burning in glass contraptions. In securing a photograph of this interesting phenomenon, I fell over a high curbstone, severely barking my shin and landing face down in a Fuschia bush. No sympathy of course: apparently it served me right for sneaking off.

It was a grand holiday and whetted our appetites for more. We would like to visit the Koblenz area of the Rhine. In spite of Solingen being the Sheffield of Germany, being a steel manufacturing centre, the countryside around is beautiful, especially the Wüpper valley, although the river itself was jet black and stinking, due to chemical contamination, which the authorities are now trying to control.

I am thinking of placing small boxes at the entrances to my

churchyards, clearly marked: "For the Deaf Jack Holiday Fund — contributions will be welcome, however small".

Some years later another grand holiday took us to Malta. No Charmian this time (now growing up and training as a nurse) just my wife and her brother, Philip.

I have a nasty suspicion that had I been travelling alone I would never have reached Malta at all. It was the first time Audrey and I had flown and the mere thought of it had been making my toes open and shut like poppet valves for weeks.

I have no doubt that seasoned travellers — even deaf ones — can find their way around with ease, calm and unflurried. I am always convinced that the train will leave early and am in a state of constant agitation until I am actually safely aboard. After that I start worrying about whether all the luggage is there, if I have the tickets/passports/bank introduction/money and so on, constantly searching my pockets to check once again, moving things from one pocket to another and panicking when something seems to be missing. Are the main services turned off, will the cat be alright in her holiday digs? Enough to drive me into a neat little detached vault...

All that and finding the way! Once we had reached Cromwell Road air terminal I relied completely on my relations for guidance and instruction and made no attempt to try and understand anything said to me by the various officials we encountered. In any case even people with normal hearing found it hard to understand what the loudspeakers were announcing. And in a place like Heathrow, a vast echoing concrete barn of a place, I couldn't understand even half of what my own party were trying to convey to me. In the day time, with the place packed with passenger traffic, it must be bedlam; we arrived at 11 o'clock at night and the plane, leaving at midnight, was the only one to leave for some hours. So it was pretty empty. Even so, there were enough people chattering, coughing, screaming and so forth to make a hearing aid quite useless.

We were passed through a metal detector, our luggage was examined in case we carried bombs or firearms, and in due course we entered the Trident. The announcements were much easier to understand in the aircraft (they were preceded by a somewhat astonishing hooting noise) and 'no smoking' and 'fasten your seatbelts' were shown on illuminated signs, thank goodness.

This is not really a travelogue so I will say little about Malta itself.

We loved the island, the people, the villages with their magnificent churches and places of interest. Had I the money I would gladly leave my churchyards from the New Year until mid-February every year and spend it in Malta.

From the hearing angle I found many of the Maltese hard to understand owing to their accented English (which was often extremely fluent). I let my family do the talking — in the churches, for example, someone always came up to show us around. The villagers were very proud of their churches and rightly so. At Mosta, the dome of the church is the third largest in the world and you could run a Mini round it — that is if you could get a Mini up there. In Gozo, the cathedral had a statue of Our Lady with a silver base which cost, I believe, ten thousand pounds. All this sort of information was relayed to me by Audrey or Philip, as in these echoing places I couldn't understand a word.

In fact our hotel was one vast echo. It was in Paradise Bay on the far north coast of Malta, still a relatively undeveloped part of the island and was built of concrete banded into the lovely honey-coloured limestone rock. It was a 'natural' for echoes, worse than any cathedral! Just sticking my key into the bedroom door sent a horde of tiny echoes shivering up and down the bare corridor, while trying to understand meal-time conversations was impossible. Even in the lounge cum bar after dinner, relatively quiet, I couldn't converse without missing fully 50% of what was said to me and eventually I gave up and wrote long letters to friends at home. There was an amusing lady from Edinburgh and her delightful daughter Fiona, who came with us on some trips in the car, two Americans and a bank manager from Exeter with his family. They would all have thought me the dimmest and dullest-witted moron in Malta had I not explained my predicament; I hope they understood! It was a time when my life-long deafness really did get me down; as a rule I don't allow it to bother me much but count my many blessings.

Another example of hearing aid drawback was thrown up in Rabat's St. Pauls Catacombs. These were 'just my cup of tea' — masses of lovely graves deep underground, cut out of the solid limestone and extending for acres, much lit up by electric light but fading into utter darkness as the excavations extend for half a mile at least under Rabat. I had wandered off by myself, taking flashlight pictures when I heard Philip calling me. I could not for the life of me, decide where he was.

34

Surrounded by graves, tunnels in all directions, his voice sounded in my ear through my aid and not from some outside point which binaural hearing would have located. I wandered about, until I finally spied Philip across an endless row of niches.

It was the same in the Hypogeum and other places. The guides' patter was always quite incomprehensible. It is better to buy guide books and leaflets and study them carefully before visiting places of interest. As well as knowing what they are about, you will know what to look for. There are some good books on Malta which a public library would obtain for you.

Do try a holiday in Malta. Go out of season if possible when the tourists are fewer but I do recommend deaf people to have a hearing friend with them. If you don't hire a car then the Valetta, Sliema and like areas would be best as buses all start from Valetta. I had the idea of hiring bicycles before we arrived in Malta but discarded this scheme on the journey to Paradise Bay in the middle of the night. We'd have been dead with fatigue long before the end of the first day. There are no mountains but plenty of terrifying hills!

"And children's voices
echo, echo, echo ---"

Oddly enough, almost indecently some people seem to think, the voices I find hardest to understand are children's -- the little dears. Choir girls aged eight to sixteen are difficult enough to take for choir practice, but with steady perseverence they can be trained to raise their voices. Tots aged three to six have me beaten every time.

For example, I am cutting a hedge with an electric trimmer driven by a petrol generator. On this job all my attention is concentrated on the trimmer — to save time and also to avoid catching my fingers in the rapidly moving blades. A small boy wanders up and we have the following conversation: "Squeak squeak" — I take no notice. "Twitter twitter" — I take no notice, he might go away again. "Chirrup chirrup" — "Oh Lor' what do you want?" "Speak chirrup twitter cheep!" — "Eh?". "WHAT ARE YOU DOING, MISTER?" At last we've arrived! Communication has been established. But do you think the little blighter keep his voice raised? Not a hope. The conversation continues: "Buzz buzz" — Ignore the nuisance again. "Snuffle snuffle HOWL!" — "Well — you shouldn't touch the engine. Of course its hot".

Trouble with small children is that they tend to repeat the question in the same words and in the same monotonous whine. When two or three of them are gathered together round me I could pick up a gravestone from sheer exasperation and tap their little heads with it.

How about my own children? They soon learnt from an early age to raise their voices when speaking to me — a habit which is obviously going to persist for the rest of their lives. There are some people who don't find it necessary to raise their voices; they have clear articulation and they don't mumble. One reason for marrying my wife; I heard with great ease the first sentences she ever spoke to me.

Most people accept my deafness and do not mind an occasional repetition of words or sentences. I have two friends who find it very difficult to come to terms with the affliction. "You didn't hear what I said!" they will say with great exasperation if I happen to miss a sentence.

The telephone is an instrument I dislike using. If it is a public call box there is the initial difficulty of understanding what the operator is saying. "Put sevatenine pence in the box please". I explain I am slightly deaf. "Put sevatenine pence in the box please". My impulse is to give up and go home. However, if it is important I persevere and await connection. Various voices come on the wire, some of which I answer, thereby muddling everyone up as my answers are unexpected and the wrong ones anyway. Eventually the receiver is lifted at the other end. A voice whispers "Hello" which I miss completely, or else I hear a sound resembling a grasshopper scratching a pimple on its back. If it is a stranger speaking he may possess a voice which sounds like an oboe with throat trouble; or it may be a lady with a squeaky voice reminding me of a mentally deranged violin. Either way I understand very little but pretend to follow perfectly, which may later lead to endless complications.

I once met a vicar to discuss levelling his churchyard. He was an undersized little shrimp of a man smoking a large cherry wood pipe. It never left his mouth for the quarter hour I was speaking to him. "Mumble mumble" would come from behind his pipe as he pointed to a curbstone. "Right, we'll shift that one", I answered cheerfully. "Mutter mutter croak croak", he'd continue while his pipe added an ecclesiastical gurgle or two. You know, I carried off the discussion with great success without having understood one word. Of course I've no idea what the vicar said to his wife when he reached home ...

A number of people stop and chat to me during the course of my churchyard work and it's most extraordinary how badly many of them speak — in low voices, barely moving their lips. I often miss three-quarters of what they say to me. If I do mention that I am slightly deaf, like as not it makes little difference. I might as well have stated that I suffered from housemaid's knee.

For television, by the way, I purchased an excellent little gadget which plugs into the back of the set — which has to be slightly adapted with a transformer. It has a long wire reaching to a control box which sits on the chair — if the cat hasn't arrived first. There is an independent volume control, a tone control switch and another switch to turn off the loudspeaker, leaving the hearing aid only in operation. For music a pair of earphones are better as the tone is vastly superior to the small earpiece speaker. I found it fascinating to be able to follow a T.V. play or film for the first time in my life.

Why, you may ask, did I lead into this dissertation with the words "And Children's Voices Echo ..."? It is a quotation from a hymn in the

English Hymnal and the line is: 'And children's voices echo answer making — Alleluia'. As far as I am concerned the nippers might as well have chanted: 'I want some water"'!

One person I used to hold long and amiable conversations with over many years, without either of us understanding a word was a real Victorian eccentric, Old Miss Hunter.

Actually, there were two Misses Hunter, Miss G.L. and Miss E. who my then eight-year-old son habitually referred to as Our Miss Hunter and Old Miss Hunter. The Rector told me that Old Miss Hunter was at her wits' end how to cope with her huge garden and that she would be overjoyed if she could find a man who could be depended on for help. She had much admired (he said) the elegant churchyard I had made for him out of his overgrown wilderness and would pay well. Welcome grist to the mill so far as I was concerned and I agreed to put in a full day every Monday.

Old Miss Hunter was 76 and was almost stone deaf. She was tall, extremely thin, with grey hair pulled back into a bun; her old-fashioned clothes hung loosely on her spare frame. She wore gold half-moon spectacles. By contrast, her sister was short, stout and very bossy". Probably Old Miss Hunter was just as bossy in her own way, but finding I was a bit deaf, and that my father had been a well-known West End dental surgeon, she decided we probably saw things from the same side of the fence (which we did) and therefore she left me alone to get on with the garden in my own way, contenting herself with suggestions when I arrived on Monday mornings, when she was always at the door to greet me.

The old lady would cup a hand behind one ear, whereupon I would shriek right into it, varying the phrases and repeating them two or three times until she understood. As she always nodded in agreement with most things I said, it became a fine art to decide whether she was nodding because she had understood — or because she had not! After my first Monday with her I was so exhausted by shouting I decided it was not possible to continue.

However, she had had such difficulty in keeping anyone (as might be understood perhaps) and was obviously going to depend on my visits, that I carried on for several years. She was somewhat eccentric and in spite of all her wealth she only cooked once a week to save fuel. She possessed an iron will; if anyone tried to make her change her mind or argue she just cut off all communication and it would be like talking, say, to a grandfather clock. She never went out and hardly saw a soul save the Rector, who had the use of her car and occasionally took her shopping to Ashford.

Although Old Miss Hunter had the reputation for being 'extremely difficult', I never had a cross word with her. The old lady was a zealous gardener and frequently we worked side by side, making conversation, quite often at cross purposes. She could never understand me unless I screamed into her ear while she had a low, flat monotonous voice caused by her near-total deafness which, with my inefficient hearing, I found difficult to understand. Once I was asking her about ordering some flowering plants and it was quite a time before I discovered she was talking about a visit to the Victoria Falls!

On several occasions I had tried to interest Old Miss Hunter in buying a hearing aid, without much success. Finally I paraded three models on the dining room table in front of her, explaining in a loud screaming voice how she would benefit from similar models. The old lady at once did her withdrawing act and mentally moved about as far away as Jupiter. No, she did not require an aid ... Yes she had tried one ... No, not recently, about 20 years ago ... It had given her head noises for a fortnight afterwards ... No, she had no intention ever of trying one again ... Very kind of you, Mr Jack, but really I don't want to hear what people say!

My hours were supposed to be from nine until four, with a break at ten-thirty precisely when she brought out a large jug of hot coffee. Old Miss Hunter was always finding reasons why I should go home early. The weather might be bad or it looked as if it might be bad before 4 o'clock. Perhaps the Folkestone Races were on and I must leave before the last race ended — this when I had moved to Hythe. Maybe I didn't look very well, possibly she didn't feel very well or else, like Garbo, she just wanted to be alone. It was never the slightest use protesting that I didn't want to go, there was too much to do, that I was enjoying myself. She would hover around, constantly popping out to see if I had packed up the tools and if not, trying to seize them herself in one grasp — spade, fork, shears, baskets, hedge trimmer and attempting to push the heavy Allen Motor Scythe with the other hand. I always had to give in rather than have her risk a heart attack.

One morning she did have an attack, while scratching up some rough grass. The doctor was sent for and she came round before he had arrived. She insisted that he be stopped; knowing his patient of course he took no notice. After the initial attack she had others of varying severity but however bad they were, she never failed to greet me on Monday mornings, although by then her hearing had really failed and we could only exchange smiles as she leaned against the door post. After some weeks she had a paralytic stroke and died the following day.

I sometimes wonder how Old Miss Hunter would have fared with the modern social services and do-gooders? (I sometimes wonder if there isn't too much talking instead of getting on with the business of finding ways of alleviating deafness).

Actually I don't really wonder about Miss Hunter at all. All social workers would have retired defeated and she'd have carried on in her own silent world (no radio, no television), happy with her garden and my weekly visits.

She was extremely anti-social and fanatically independent — I suspect both qualities were there before deafness hit her; isolation merely accentuated them. Dear Miss Hunter! You left me a handsome legacy but more than that, an affectionate memory of a real Victorian eccentric.

Hobbies

Life is not all churchyarding and lawn mowing. Some of my other interests are well-suited for the deaf., Church architecture, local history, polishing pebbles and semi-precious stones, looking for underground tunnels and caving ... And to retain memories and have records of all these things, photography is an ideal hobby for deaf people, I believe, so long as one does it oneself.

The original Kodak slogan by which many photographers still live: 'You Press the Button, We do the Rest' (circa 1900) gives all the real fun and excitement to others. Watching the first positive image growing up faintly from the bottom of your own developing dish in the bright orange glow of a safelight is, in miniature, as thrilling as the explorer's glimpse of an unknown land. Few places are so snug, so restful, free from distraction, questioning, argument, as your own darkroom.

For snapshotters almost any camera will do — the simpler the better; a useful adjunct is an automatic exposure meter which relieves the simpler-minded from the worry of deciding 'how long to give it'. Since my photography can include anything from long distance shots to close-up copying of documents, copy slides, taking pictures in restricted places, I use single lens reflex cameras; two similar models so that the telephoto and wide angle lenses fit both cameras. Since the exposure meter views the scene through the actual taking lens there is never any difficulty, however varied the subject matter.

One does not have to be a photographer, of course, to be interested in church architecture. Instead of imitating so many visitors who whip round a church in 10 minutes or less (I know — I watch 'em!) why not make yourself an expert? One aspect of a church may appeal to you; perhaps the various sorts of enrichment, in certain styles of architecture — Norman, Decorated, and so on. Maybe stained glass interests you? Then take a pair of binoculars and view the stained windows through them. It is a revelation! They make beautiful transparencies once the knack of judging the exposure has been caught.

The study of a church is again a sort of detective work, puzzling out how the building has evolved into its present shape. Our country is fortunate in possessing an unrivalled series of ecclesiastical buildings, from humble Saxon and Norman village churches to the great cathedrals and ruined abbeys. Did you know that the choir of Canterbury Cathedral is basically French, and why?

An aspect of churches which I intend to capture one day are the many gargoyles and odd little faces scattered around, some quaintly humorous. Besides acting as water spouts, they are found at the sides of archways and doorways, sometimes at the end of pews. There are some marvellous gargoyles on Notre Dame in Paris, but many fine ones too nearer home.

Of course I use my camera for family records and holidays as well as to illustrate some of my articles. Or else I see something of interest, take a good picture, or an unusual viewpoint, write a caption and sell it. It may involve a bit of research in the reference library.

The point which I hope I have made about these hobbies is that it is better to become immersed in them and not just dabble! In a phrase, use your intellect.

As regards books for reading, your public library will have plenty from which to choose, but when one particularly takes your fancy, buy it. Read a series of books on the same subject and distill the information which most interests you — write it down, make extracts or an index — that in itself can become a hobby. In Kent, Igglesden's 'Saunters through Kent with Pen and Pencil' were an invaluable starting point for me; thirty volumes full of local history, legends and facts. (But I don't suggest buying that lot!) There is the Shire series of books aptly written by local authors, full of interesting details. Messrs. Batsford publish a very fine series of books, profusely illustrated, on all aspects of ecclesiastical architecture.

My own feeling is that as one grows older and then retires from a full-time occupation, it is necessary to have some worthwhile mental interest (and combined with physical activity if need be) or the mind stagnates and one ages prematurely. Better to be an active bore discoursing on the latest obscure stained glass saint you've just found than a vegetable only concerned with eating and sleeping.

My interest in the subterranean world started when I read some books by an archaeologist, the late Tom Lethbridge, in which he explained the use of a divining rod or a pendulum to discover burial sites, filled-in ditches and the like.

Most people know vaguely that by holding a forked hazel stick many people are able to find water. It isn't only water. It is possible to dowse for coal, oil, metal ores, buried treasure — anything beneath the surface. To go a step further, it is not necessary to be at the actual site. It is much more convenient to swing a pendulum over a map of the site at home and gain the required information; a visit to the site should enable you to go straight to the right place and verify your homework.

I have no idea how it works — on the site, yes, it is either some electrical force given off by the object (as running water) or else one is detecting a discontinuity in the earth's magnetic field. But to draw a rough quick map with a ball pen, then to swing a pendulum over it and find out where the drains are — that seems like a sort of magic! I am sure unknown laws of nature are at work and maybe one day we shall understand them.

One can use either a 'short pendulum' about four inches long or adjust its length according to your search. This means a 7½" pendulum for cavities or 22" for silver.

Reading instructions on how to operate a forked stick was easy but applying them in practice did not work. Later I was asked to visit an artist and take colour photographs of his paintings; in the course of conversation the topic of dowsing came up, it being much in my mind at the time. A professional water diviner had shown my new friend how to do it. We went into his garden and he cut a forked stick from his hazel hedge. His garden was on a slope and one corner had a filled-in pond, although I was unaware of this fact at the time. He demonstrated the way to hold the stick and he moved slowing along the slope. To my enormous interest, the stick slowly moved backwards towards him and tilted downward. I took the stick, feeling, it must be confessed, rather a fool and walked across the garden. To my astonishment I felt the stick moving and it slowly turned downward. I felt quite unable to hold it still and gained the impression it would have broken or pulled skin off my palms had I seriously tried to impede it. Being absolutely overcome by finding I had the gift and quite excited, I rushed over and kissed my artist friend's wife — who most fortunately happened to be young and pretty!

Having established the fact that I had some sort of gift for dowsing, I hastened to apply it to underground tunnels and vaults. I might explain here that you must carry in your hand a 'witness' of whatever you are seeking. If coal, a bit of coal; if the foundations of an old building, brick, perhaps, or you might be seeking old pottery or coins. (For water no witness is needed since we are mostly made of water.) For empty spaces underground one carries a small empty bottle — as a scent vial — something conveniently tucked in the palm along with the stick. (Well, carry a Kilner jar if you have hands like King Kong!) The emptiness of the bottle is to remind you mentally you wish to resonate with empty pace. There are those who consider that the witness itself has some effect on the dowsing.

The first thing I did was to test it on a known graveyard vault, which gave a positive reaction. One of my churchyards is supposed to have a secret passage under it, leading from the tower to an ancient hotel nearby — we had actually been down the start of this passage in the hotel cellar. I walked back and forth over the churchyard at right angles over the rough area where the passage was supposed to lie. A regular series of reactions resulted; at each one a stick was pushed in the ground and at the end of the experiment I had a line of sticks from hotel to church tower.

I had in the meantime taught the trick to my medical student son who later tested the churchyard quite independently and obtained substantially the same line as I had done. You can also detect vaults under church floors.

Certain things seem to inhibit the 'flow of resonance' such as plastics and perhaps tarmacadam surfaces.

People are apt to comment that this business is connected with ghosts and other psychic phenomena. It is, of course, nothing whatever to do with spiritualism! It seems to utilise some little known power of the human brain, akin perhaps to telepathy or ESP. (Telepathy operates whether the distance is 5 yards or 5000 miles.) Like many brain processes this dowsing improves with practice. A sensitive agent will sense water with no external aids at all; others can find water (or oil or enemy mines in the Thames estuary) merely by using maps on a bigger and bigger scale until the area can be pin-pointed. By sitting in a room in Surrey it is possible to trace minerals in far-off Africa!

It is safe to say that auto-suggestion can play a part in the dowsing process and it has to be guarded against. On the other hand on several occasions I have had unexpected negative reactions or vice-versa. Recently I was sitting in a hotel sitting room explaining dowsing to a professional medium who, oddly enough, had never tried it. I casually held a stick in the correct position with a small bottle tucked in my palm and continued chatting. Presently the stick began to dip slowly downward but away from me instead of towards me as it invariably

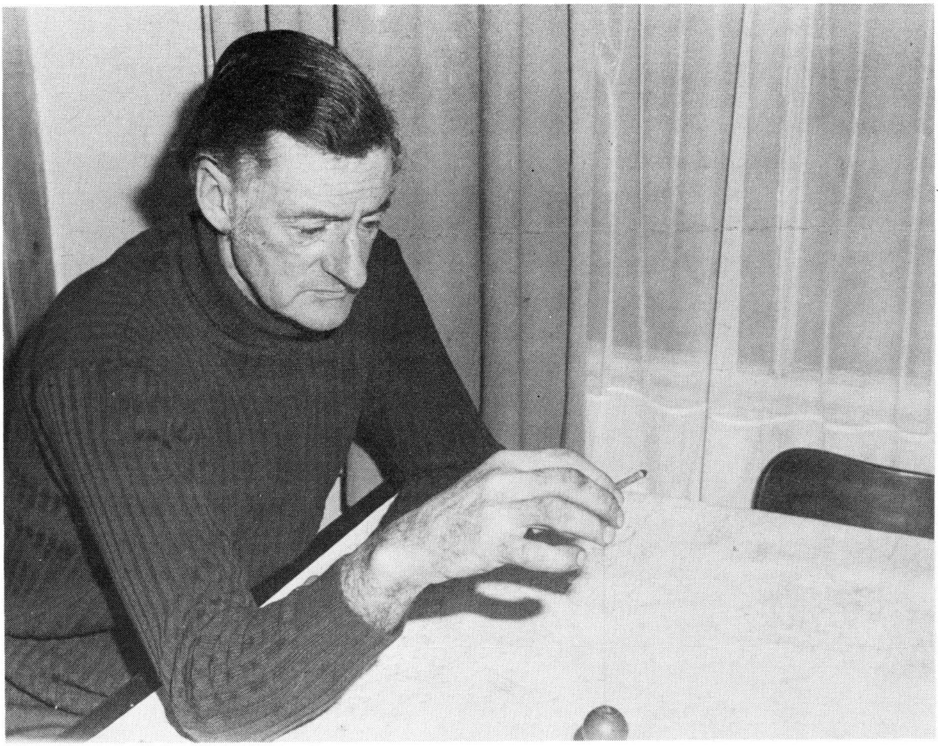

*The author
dowsing for tunnels
with a 7¹/₂ in.
pendulum*

*The author showing
that a spiral force
travels up standing
stones and it will
throw off a dowser
clinging to it*

45

Charmian looking at skulls in the world famous crypt in Hythe, Kent.

The author down the 1880 Channel Tunnel near Folkestone

46

does. A moment's thought showed us that the hotel basement was below us; we were sitting in the window and the stick was attracted towards the empty space below and in front of us.

The grip is important; palm uppermost, the thin ends of the fork one in each hand, the little fingers pressing down and exerting the necessary pressure. The Y stems ideally should be of equal thickness and leave the stem at equal angles; unequal arms are liable to produce lop-sidedness. Hazel forks naturally but it isn't easy to find perfect forks — about the thickness of a pencil. It does not have to be hazel; other flexible woods such as willow and hornbeam can be used successfully. For cavities I usually use a yard-long piece of water pipe balanced in the palm of my hand which dips downward on reaching a tunnel or other underground structure.

I soon found that Kent is simply riddled with tunnels: they pop up all over the place. For example, when I first started churchyarding and was cutting Bekesbourne churchyard near Canterbury, an old lady told me that her husband had been working on the site of the old Archbishop's palace, demolished 300 years ago or so; he fell into a hole, found himself in a tunnel, walked along it and came up in Canterbury cathedral! About three miles as the crow flies.

I intended writing up this area with a history of the old palace, formerly connected with Christchurch (the cathedral) but for nineteen years I put it off until I finally went to the house to ask the owner if I might take some photographs. It turned out that he had heard of the tunnel legend (though not my story). Furthermore, he added, main drainage was about to be laid through his garden and if the tunnel was there it would surely turn up. I swung my 7½ inch pendulum over a 2½ inch ordnance map of the area and it showed a tunnel running through the old palace garden. A few days later the owner phoned to say my tunnel had been found about where I predicted.

About 10 years ago, soon after moving to a new house, I began to feel very queer. Looking back, it must have been a near collapse from working too hard for so long, or so the doctors might say, or perhaps it was my age — 51. I decided it was caused by sleeping over running water, recalling that from the moment we moved I began sleeping badly. Somewhere I had read that sleeping over moving water is very bad for some sensitive people, because the water conducts away their nervous energy: it may also cause rheumatism, arthritis and kindred ailments.

I went to my local doctor who gave me a quick check-up lasting five minutes (which is all any medico has time for nowadays) and he said I was in fine shape. This did not prevent me having a feeling of wearing a tight cap around my head, waking up in the night thinking I was paralysed or perhaps to find myself bathed in sweat, with it trickling off my face — all very beastly. And as this was happening several times a week, naturally I got the wind up!

Feeling rather worse five months later and my local doctor obviously being quite uninterested, although I had returned again, I decided to get advice from an old family friend who had become Head of Medicine in the Middlesex Hospital. Not only did my father qualify there, I did a stint as a medical student myself there, and my daughter had just started nursing in the same hospital. If the Professor of Medicine couldn't find out what was wrong with me, who could?

He very kindly gave me a private appointment and a thorough overhaul which lasted well over half an hour. All my reflexes were tested for a start; I didn't even know I possessed some of them — and my arms, legs, feet, ears and perhaps even eyeballs were twitching or rolling as they were tapped, scratched, stuck with pins or dusted with cotton wool!

Anyway, although there would be blood and specimen tests and X-rays, it looked as if I was superlatively fit — caused, no doubt, by nineteen years' hard churchyarding labour. The blood test, contrary to my expectations, did not hurt. "Now wait a minute ..." I began to say, as the operator brought a fat syringe near my arm, and the next second it was full of blood — my blood, dash it!

The X-rays, apart from normal checks for TB, were to see if I had any injury from a fall on my neck two years previously. Possible 'cervical sponylosis' it said on my X-ray card, which sounded a pretty rotten sort of thing to have. I was very careful never to ask what it was before my X-rays (which as it turned out were quite all right) and afterwards I had forgotten about it. The whole business was quite a cliff-hanger because of course one wonders if something is going to show up which no-one had ever suspected — a lucky brass charm, perhaps, swallowed as a baby, which over the years had worked its way round behind my ear.

The staff took five shots, then sent me back to get dressed and await the developing and assessment of the plates. After twenty minutes the operator put her head round the door and said another shot was needed — would I de-shirt myself again? Like music in the thrillers, my mental orchestra began to play, violins screaming and tympani going bim bim bim boom!! (Beethoven's Fifth, as if you didn't know).

What had they found? Another X-ray and another wait ... again the operator put her head round the door. Yet another shot must be taken! This was it: hastily I began to compose an epitaph — Here lies Michael Jack, a noted collector of churchyards ... But seeing my expression the nurse said hastily it wasn't me, just that the first pictures were not clear enough.

After all that, two more X-rays were taken on my next visit. I had suggested unkindly that perhaps the machine could be thoroughly overhauled by a reliable expert before tackling my anatomy again. I suspect this little quip was not regarded with much amusement; anyway, this time I was treated to a different machine altogether! They had the nerve to suggest that my shoulders were on the thick side — or did they mean my head?

My Professor of Medicine friend made an appointment with their neurologist to find out where my pins and needles were starting. He was a decent sort with a good sense of humour. "Churchyard Consultant?" he said incredulously, staring at me as though I said I'd come from the moon. I explained, adding that I covered an area from Northiam in Sussex across to Whitstable on the north Kent coast. "Northiam?" repeated the neurologist, "I live there". "Hah! then you'll be one of my little flock there, one day", I pointed out triumphantly. He took it very well. Not really the sort of thing West End neurologists expect on the National Health.

Pins and needles, as it turned out, were an occupational hazard brought on by vibration from the motor mowers irritating the nerve running down in front of the wrist. Though in fact, as my health grew better the pins and needles gradually grew less in intensity.

Reassured over my excellent state, I next turned my attention to this business of running water under the bedroom. (The Professor, of course, considered it the barmiest idea he'd ever heard of and told me to forget it immediately).

Dowsing with a hazel Y stick or a pendulum showed clearly that a fount of water was coming from under the passage outside our bedroom, ran through the room under the bed area, across our drive and probably down to the Enbrook Valley adjoining the property, a place so full of water that the local authority had to abandon a prospective school site after spending several thousand pounds on it. The stream did not seem to affect our daughter's room on the opposite side of the passage. Our room is twenty-one feet long and some more dowsing showed the western end to be free from subterranean aquatic activity.

The obvious thing was to move the bed to the other side of the room. I had woken up, as usual, one night, but this time got out of bed, dragged out a mattress from under the bed to the other side of the room, added a car rug and my overcoat and had gone to sleep on the floor, shaking with laughter at the absurdity of the situation! The next time I moved into my daughter's room, Charmian being in the hospital at the time. I didn't laugh, since I had given myself only an hour or two of life ... in fact I nearly went down to get my churchyard accounts straight. Only I fell asleep first.

After this I moved the bed to the new position and we've been there ever since, thus proving to my own satisfaction at any rate, that my trouble was due to the underground stream.

What, you will certainly ask, did my wife make of all this hoo-ha? Well, we had been married twenty-eight years so none of it really surprised her. She is strictly practical with none of my odd little notions but she was quite willing to go along with my ideas if it stopped me from either dropping off my perch or becoming actively dangerous.

Once when cutting Adisham churchyard I heard someone playing the organ. On entering, the church proved empty. I peered under the organ bench in case a little man two feet high was hiding there and even under the organ pedals in case an even smaller little man two inches high was hiding, but there wasn't. You may prefer prosaic explanations: I look for psychic causes.

Anyone writing on this sort of topic, on psychical matters or healing, runs the risk of being dubbed a crank but, supremely convinced of the truth of all these things from my own practical experience, I am quite indifferent to the opinions expressed by the unenlightened.

You might say, I suppose, that my one venture on the fringe of politics came under the heading of a hobby. With the astonishing exception of Jack Ashley (who had made it to the top anyway before he was struck) I doubt if any truly deaf man has succeeded in this noisy and difficult arena.

It was only a fringe job for me anyway — canvassing in a by-election. An elderly lady friend of mine had asked me if I would go up to London and help a young friend of hers. Of course I said No! I had no intention of knocking on doors and arguing politics with total strangers; the mere thought made my toes curl up and down.

However, my friend was very persuasive. She was sure there was something I could do not involving a lot of listening. And wouldn't it be nice to have a change from my churchyards? A little less ghoulish perhaps? Yes?

A few days later I was introduced to the candidate in her S.E. London committee rooms. As a matter of fact she was a strikingly pretty young lady; my enthusiasm for her cause went up several points. My friend said, in the inevitable stage whisper: "Mr Jack is slightly deaf". The usual reaction — the candidate took a quick backward step and an expression of alarm flickered over her attractive features. A brain which lacked proper hearing might well slip a few more cogs and cause its owner to become actively dangerous. I could read her mind like a book. "What would Mr. Jack like to do?" her agent asked loudly and nervously. Note they didn't dare ask me directly. "Anything not involving conversation", I stated firmly. When it was understood that I was an experienced car driver I was sent with another helper to fetch the election vehicle. We started off to the garage, my companion carrying a mysterious black box. On reaching the main shopping centre he stopped and opened up the box. It was a portable loud hailer.

Applying his mouth to the microphone he announced the many virtues of the candidate in a stentorian bellow. I did not much care for this and stared rigidly into a shop window, pretending to be quite unconnected with the performance. There was no need to have worried as no-one took the slightest notice of his performance.

The election vehicle gave me a very nasty shock. It was an ancient limousine — about twice as big as a hearse. If the sheer size hadn't daunted me the knock-out blow was provided by the gigantic seven-foot placards fastened to each side.

A mechanic drifted up, a cigarette hanging from the corner of his mouth and gave me his opinion of the car. I failed to catch much of his mutter — a certain six-letter word was repeated pretty often, but I gathered he thought I was a right plucked 'un to take the vehicle on the road. That made two of us.

I climbed the equivalent of the Matterhorn into the driving seat.

After only 10 minutes I had the engine firing on seven of its eight cylinders. The dashboard held nearly as many instruments as a jet air liner and I never discovered what three-quarters of them were for. This didn't matter as none were in working order except the radiator thermometer.

There was no licence. Loud hailer, on being appealed to, insisted that it was almost certainly licensed. Insurance? He hissed sharply through his teeth. Well, he was almost certain it was insured — couldn't be sure, look you man, but they had said something about it in the office ten days ago.

I was required to pick up a load of canvassers and drop them off at various places in the constituency. We were accompanied by a continual grating and crashing of gears. My respect for the olde-tyme driving veterans without synchromesh increased considerably.

Dropping off the last canvasser I was left with a pile of leaflets and instructions to post one through every letter-box in my allotted area — two streets of quite inordinate length. ("You need not talk to people if you don't want to", was the candidate's parting shot).

My one idea was to avoid all contact with my fellow mortals and thus avoid political argument. I intended to steal quietly up the garden path, slip a leaflet through the letter-box and move off before anyone came to the door. The entire business, in fact, was to be conducted with as little uproar as a transient jelly-fish.

This excellent plan broke down at the very first house. A curtain was twitched aside as I sneaked up the path and my fingers had hardly tested the letter flap when the door flew open. A large fat women dressed entirely in black confronted me. "'Ere! 'Ow long is that owld car stopping ahtside me 'ouse?" I need not have worried about hearing her; she spoke in a hoarse bellow. I applied some soothing oil — "Hardly any time my dear lady, perhaps half an hour?" "An p'haps it ain't." She stabbed a stumpy finger at my head — "I got a funeral in 'arf an hour and I don't want no nasty bag of tricks with them boards stopping ahtside my 'ouse".

Remembering I was the candidate's representative, I delivered a beautiful apology. Handing over a leaflet I hastily shambled back down the garden path. "'An I don't want no leaflets neither," the good madam bawled after my retreating figure. "Yer candidate's subversive, that's what — subversive. Lucky fer you me old man ain't at 'ome!"

Possibly Messrs Heath, Wilson or Mrs Thatcher could have dealt with it. As a canvasser I was way down in the fourth division. Parking the car further down the road, I hoped fervently there had not been any further deaths.

Trotting from house to house like a bee fertilising flowers, I left my leaflets and clapped on an extra burst of speed if I heard footsteps approaching the doors.

Presently it began to drizzle and then to rain. I tucked a small pile of soggy leaflets under my raincoat and jamming my hat over my eyebrows to shoot the rain off my face, I walked into a pair of iron gates.

The kind of place which would obviously vote Conservative, still, they might as well have the benefit of my reading matter. My head still lowered I passed between the gates, not bothering to look up until I had fallen over a gravestone. It was the local cemetery. Back in the usual routine — graveyards and funerals!

Calling it a day I collected the election vehicle and drove back to GHQ, picking up a load of sodden canvassers on the way. A particularly bad bout of gear changing caused a learner-driver to stop and wave me on.

The candidate was effusively thankful and gave me the impression that if she became an M.P. it would be entirely due to my devoted canvassing.

Pretty as she was, alas, she came at the bottom of the poll!

Funerals and Christmas

Writing about my canvassing (where I ended up in the local cemetery), reminds me how the attitude to cremation has changed, a change which began round about the time I started my business in 1953.

Near Canterbury is the splendid village of Ickham and one of my earliest jobs was to cut the churchyard and a piece of ground behind it, in readiness for the bishop to consecrate the latter as the new burial ground. It was a largish area as originally laid out and after all these years it has only a handful of graves. Cremation started becoming more fashionable — I believe nowadays about 70% of funerals are followed by cremation. I know a Roman Catholic priest who would not consider cremation in the middle fifties ("a pagan custom") but a few years later many of his parishioners were being cremated.

One thinks of huge areas filled with thousands of graves — Highgate has 50,000 graves crammed into thirty-five acres in the old area. Acres of ground not only useless for any other purpose but also needing huge sums of money to keep more or less tidy. I hate to think how much more land would have been needed had inhumation continued on its old scale.

This cremation topic prompts me to relate one of the more macabre hilarities of my life — the day we cremated my Great Aunt Alexandra. Time might have blunted the finer points of my memory, but in retrospect it went something like this*.

She was a great eccentric all her life, and I fear (being psychic) still is after her death. There are times when I am absolutely certain Great Aunt Alexandra is still buzzing about the place, emanating disapproval and silent, sarcastic comment.

The main trouble was that she did not want to be cremated and had said so loudly and frequently to anyone unwise enough to listen to her. Neither had she any wish to be buried in our new cemetery. "All that nasty new grass and that miserable wretch Harry Snodkin doddering about trying to keep it tidy — no thank you, Vicar! Let me lie in peace in a wee corner of our ancient churchyard with the wild grasses waving over me", she added dramatically with a carefully contrived dry sob.

*The events relating to her demise are partly fiction, partly fact, but based on a real funeral. Which is which, is left to the reader's own imagination.

The vicar pointed out that the old churchyard was closed and therefore no further burials could take place. 'It was an Order in Council", he added firmly, thinking this would hold great-aunt. "Ridiculous!" she had snorted. "Then tell the Council to make another Order, opening it up for me". After he had pointed out that this was impossible, the vicar was dismissed as a weak-kneed cleric. As he was called something like this twice a week he took no notice and suggested cremation instead.

This really stirred great-aunt. She'd spent 80 years on this earth, we were told and she was not going to leave it as a heap of cinders. Anyway, she said, just look at her — look at her! We did so in awe and respect, all 17 stone of her. How, she demanded, did we expect the machine to cope with her bulk? The vicar assured her, perhaps tactlessly, that the ovens were capable of cremating anyone — "Even an elephant!" he muttered to us and winked. Aunt Alexandra was supposed to be very deaf but refused any sort of hearing aid (I don't need one!). Unfortunately she heard the vicar's little quip; it took three heart pills to get her back to normal ...

We pointed out that if she was buried there might be a mistake with the certificate ... Dr. Whosit, she agreed, was certainly capable of certifying death in a live electric wire. We pointed out in jocular fashion that if she wasn't perfectly dead when she entered the crematorium she certainly would be soon afterwards! We left the room in a hurry with a small china ornament whizzing past our ears.

The first crisis came shortly after her death. The local undertaker was a little shrimp of a fellow and he worried about getting great-aunt downstairs, fearing she might get stuck, since her stairs were narrow with a sharp bend in the middle.

"Very inconvenient", he pointed out. "If the — um — deceased is blocking the staircase, how will you manage?" We suggested he carried her downstairs like a sack of potatoes but this merely made him laugh. Had we ever tried lifting a 17-stone sack of potatoes? We hadn't. Eventually the window frame was removed and the coffin was lowered (with great-aunt inside) on stout ropes.

The time for the funeral arrived and we duly lined up in our cars behind the hearse. We had naturally been extremely careful never to mention cremation in the house. Great-aunt Alexandra's indomitable will and irasicible nature had made her feared for miles around and although she might be dead, her influence lingered on. Also, freed from the encumbrances of the flesh, her hearing might have sharpened up very considerably; we took no chances.

We had a suspicion that she might be aware of what was happening when the hearse broke down at the corner of our road and when this was speedily put right, a tyre was found to be flat. Eventually we reached the crematorium 20 minutes late — great-aunt was never late — and found a worried verger waiting on the steps. "About that there music you ordered", he said to me, "I'm afraid I can't do nothing about it."

It seems he had started to wind back the pre-recorded tape of organ music and turned his back — only for a second, guv'nor — to find the tape a tangled mess on the floor and chewed up beyond all redemption. Couldn't understand how it had all happened, he couldn't. We could, all too easily.

Our great-aunt had detested tape recorders, ever since the day one of the children had recorded her voice. She had never sounded like that — why it was a downright nasty common voice that came out of the machine!

I suggested we had the organ instead and I would play it myself, but no, the blower had caught fire the previous afternoon.

The service was conducted therefore with no music. The vicar appeared understandably nervous. He had suffered a great deal from great-aunt's volcanic eruptions in her lifetime and the habit lingered. However, all went without a hitch until the part where the coffin is supposed to slide through the little velvet curtains.

Then:— There was a faint click and a humming and the coffin began to slide through the curtains. Half-way through, the humming stopped — and so did great aunt. It looked as though the vicar's dismissal had been inefficient. So often she had called him a nit-witted addle-pated cleric; maybe there could have been a grain of truth in her assertions?

Before the vicar could pull himself together and repeat the dismissal, great aunt slowly came back into the chapel, followed by a hand which seized the coffin and dragged it out of sight. The old lady had finally reached the end of her journey. After all the other odd little incidents, a little matter of the roller mechanism fusing might almost have been expected!

We eventually received the ashes in a dignified little aluminium urn and the question then arose where were they to be kept? It was suggested keeping the urn on the piano, of which she was very fond. But, as my wife pointed out, suppose the urn fell on the floor? What a crowning indignity if great-aunt's mortal remains were sucked up into a vacuum cleaner bag!

The vicar solved the problem finally by offering to bury the ashes in the old churchyard. The ashes, as he pointed out, were perfectly hygienic. We trembled ... suppose great-aunt had overheard him? "Hygienic! Me — hygienic? I always said the man was a perfect fool!"

My earliest memories seem quite unaffected by my deafness, except that I couldn't hear things like far-off church bells or trains, bird and animal noises or the ticking of clocks. In fact I don't remember missing my proper hearing as a child. But recently my oldest girl friend was here and as we had been brought up together I asked if she had noted my deafness when we were very small. She nodded her head and said it had been very obvious. We tend to remember the good things and forget the bad, or push them away to a corner of the subconscious mind.

The happiest holiday of my young days was in 1936 when I was sixteen and we spent a week in a hotel at Barton-on-Sea. We were joined by my dearest girl friend and her family and there were dances every evening — 'The Way You Look Tonight' was my favourite dance tune — walks and countless encounters with Pam under the mistletoe in the daytime. On the last evening Pam came in to say goodnight and I told her I loved her (as if she didn't know!)

Later that night my mother came rushing in: "Michael! Get up quickly! The hotel is on fire!" By golly! I've never in my life got out of bed so quickly ... I had not, of course, been woken by the fire bell. Most of the guests were already standing about in various stages of night attire and we were amused to see that some of the ladies did not appear for quite a long time as they thought it necessary to make up their faces and do their hair before appearing in public, fire or no fire.

With a new vicar in 1953 I went along to the early communion service at seven o'clock on Christmas Day to play three hymns. It meant entering the church in the darkness, turning on the church and Christmas tree lights and donning cassock and surplice. Just before seven, as a congregation was silently assembling, I started playing very quietly. This brings back memories of magical quality; slow reflective organ music stealing through the lit-up church, bright with decorations, the feeling of festal happiness in the air and then the first hymn with full organ on the last refrain — "O come let us adore Him, Christ the Lord!"

Then a minute's walk home for breakfast and the two young boys opening their presents. In 1953 they were joined by a sister (and as I write this, my wife has gone baby-sitting for that same daughter's baby, now three years old). Deafness has never seemed a handicap at Christmas time — which, above all, is a family occasion and my family are used to my hearing problems. With the churchyarding business starting in 1953 it was possible to spend two or three days at home with the family and have a proper break — no cows to milk, pigs and chickens to feed. Just the organ playing, always a pleasure, with the two boys in the choir.

One Christmas Day which stands out is 1970, our first in our wing of this Kent manor house where we still live (there has been a house on this site since 1150). With plenty of room, we were able to have all the family for Christmas lunch, the first time together since my mother died ten years before. She had always been a great one for family parties and as I started carving the turkey I became aware she was standing right beside me.

I must digress here to explain that we all possess an electric field or it might be the aura, and when another person enters it there is some alteration in the shape — as when iron filings on a piece of paper over a magnet will arrange themselves in a pattern. Bring another magnet close and the pattern is altered. Most people have experienced a creepy feeling when alone in a room and someone comes in unobserved and is looking at them. The fact that this other person may be physically dead does not appear to stop them possessing a magnetic field and therefore my mother, standing beside me, made her presence felt although unseen. It lasted several minutes and then faded away, leaving me shaking and almost unable to continue carving the turkey.

Hearing Aids and Reactions

Hearing aids are a great boon and I would hate to be without my behind-ear aid. You will remember I started off with a Medresco and I have also mentioned the aid incorporated in a pair of glasses. Best of all, for me, is the behind-ear aid. A customer offered me his behind-ear aid when he bought a new one and in return I mowed his lawn for the rest of the season — it turned out to be a wet one which was tiresome.

Since then I have bought several aids. One had an extra — a 'basi-cut' — which, on being brought into operation, cut out the low tones, the idea being that it cut out background noise and let you hear your conversationalist more clearly. I found it useless as it made everything sound like five Irish starlings talking politics.

Some hearing aids did not have a shielded microphone so that the slightest breeze sent it completely berserk. The frontally-placed microphone seems better while I believe there are more sophisticated models now which have automatic volume control which means that sudden loud sounds are automatically by-passed. This would be useful for a church organist faced with the problem of hearing a parson some distance away and then his organ and choir nearby. I always have to keep twiddling the volume control either to boost the parson's voice or to soften the music, which is a bother, especially when playing responses.

Sometimes I wonder how recently deafened musicians cope with choir training. Do years of practice enable them to carry on by using a hearing aid? I found out once that even musicians with good hearing cannot always pick out choral mistakes. I spent a week at the Royal School of Church Music on a choir training course. One exercise was to conduct a choir practice with the rest of the class as guinea pigs. Three of us at the back consistently sang a bass part different from the printed line in one hymn. At the end of the practice Dr. Willis Grant, then organist of Birmingham Cathedral, summed up the class' effort and added caustically (with a baleful glare in our direction) that three gentlemen at the back sang an entirely different bass part in the hymn but none of you noticed the fact! So doubtless good hearing is not sufficient; it needs training and practice and I daresay many hard of hearing choir trainers cope as efficiently as their hearing colleagues.

One of the greatest drawbacks is the way the aid presents all sounds reaching it. Listening to a conversation in a crowded room the normal hearing person can concentrate on what he wants to hear and relegate the rest to the background. This is much more difficult to do with an aid but it can be done, with practice. Though I remember a recent sherry party with thirty people crammed into one room, I took off my aid and got on much better without it but everyone was shouting anyway.

And of course the sound comes from within the ear and not from its point of origin. For example, I was crossing the Sittingbourne/Isle of Sheppey road last summer with a load of tools to subdue Bobbing churchyard. A sudden sharp 'toot!' sounded in my ear. Quite unable to tell where it came from, I glanced round towards Sheppey and was nearly knocked flat by a car coming from Sittingbourne. Almost a candidate for one of my own churchyards.

Though actually I'm going to be cremated when my time comes — not, of course, before then. It's in my Will. When I made my Will my lawyer asked if I wanted to be buried or cremated. Well, what with one thing and another I hadn't given much thought to the subject from a personal angle, but burial seemed nice; lying peacefully with some other churchyarding type toiling away above me.. but one might Wake Up!! Could be a very nasty situation indeed. So I decided on cremation since even if the doctor did have an off-day and slip up, there wasn't much life in a pot of ashes. The heat might be uncomfortable for a few minutes ... how about the vultures, as in India? Vultures don't flap around free in this country, as my lawyer cleverly pointed out, so it's going to be cremation.

It is not until an aid becomes necessary that one realises how wonderful and adaptable the human ear can be. A normal hearing person can listen to his watch ticking, then he can look up and face the full blast from an orchestra of a hundred players. If, at this moment, I wanted to hear my watch ticking I should have to put on my hearing aid and turn it up until it was ready to howl with resentment. Then if our cuckoo clock happens to get cracking at the same time, it sounds ten times louder and six times more aggressive than a hawk catching a pigeon.

I was mowing Wye churchyard the other day while a wedding was taking place in the church. A perfectly delightful young thing wandered by, waiting for the bridal party to emerge; she had a ready smile and was wearing scarlet slacks and a tight white jumper, which caused the mower to lose power and stop as she came along. We fell into conversation and as her voice was low and sweet, I just turned up the aid volume and heard her perfectly. We were deep in a discussion of sweet nothings when the end of the world started up inside my head … or so it seemed for an agonising five seconds until I had turned down the volume and realised that the bell ringers had swung into action.

Much of my work is concerned with mowing lawns for older people. With advancing years some of my customers have lost their hearing and resorted to hearing aids; it is clear that many old folk cannot get adjusted to them or get the best possible use out of them. I have in mind one old chap who bought a behind-ear aid a couple of years ago. I was having a cup of tea with him after mowing the lawn and obtaining some queer answers to my questions I looked and saw he had no aid on. "No b....y use — it deafens me!" He then produced it. Of course it deafened him. The volume control was full on. (Separate on/ off switch.) I explained about the control, speaking in a thin screech which took pounds off the value of my voice-box but all to no avail, he couldn't understand what I was driving at and neither could his very sensible daughter. I had to explain it was just like a radio and the volume was turned according to the output needed.

The old fellow is now much more doddery and while I was mowing the lawn this summer he was brought out and settled in a deck chair with two drinks — one for me, one for him. He now spoke in a low harsh croak which was difficult to interpret since turning up my aid merely resulted in a louder harsher croak. Again he couldn't hear me. "You aren't wearing your aid!" I said loudly. "You haven't got your hearing aid on!!" I yelled, thereby causing a sleeping cat next door to wake up with a start and scoot indoors. "No b....y good!" he croaked. His daughter brought it out and fitted it to his ear — "Is that better?" "No!!" She turned up the volume and the result depressed him still further. He had a Medresco, she said, would I put in a new battery for her? I prised off the battery lid and peered inside. There was a fluffy white cylinder with beautiful green crystals at each end … it took a screwdriver to lever it out. After cleaning up the terminals and inserting the new battery I gave the Medresco to the daughter who fitted it into the old gentleman's left ear, the right ear still having the private aid in it. She was having such shocking difficulty fitting it in that I looked to see what the trouble was — hardly surprising as it was a right ear mould. So the private aid was taken off and the Medresco mould put in its place. It fitted rather worse than a dried pea in a broad bean pod. "He'll need a new ear-piece — that is a mouldy fit, I fear". Then I collected my money and took my departure before the clever little pun had sunk in — if indeed it ever did.

The chief effect of my deafness, apart from a general lowering of the auditory level, is to reduce my capacity for hearing the higher pitched sounds. While people with normal hearing have a constant level which falls off slightly towards the very high notes (and is aggravated by advancing age), my hearing level starts at a lower stage and soon drops smartly down towards the mat. If I play a musical scale on the piano it becomes impossible to hear any note much over two octaves above middle C. This would be around 1024 cycles per second, or Hz as the moderns have it.

Having stated these facts let me now consider their implications. Consider an orchestral concert with its assortment of instruments from the double bass sounding two octaves below middle C to small flutes and violins sounding several octaves above. Since I am unable to hear the full range of the higher pitched instruments (which comes harder with the distance), my appreciation of the music is totally unbalanced. the lower notes — to which I am more sensitive are disporportionately loud while, unable to hear the high notes, I cannot follow the progress of the music and a sense of tune, of continuity in the musical progress, is completely lost. Indeed, a hearing listener suddenly presented with the same aural reception would probably dismiss the music as a grotesque caricature of the real thing. As far as appreciating a violin or flute concerto, I might as well stay at home and play tiddly-winks.

This affects musical recognition. The other day, my wife heard me pick up a bar of music while I twiddled the radio tuning knob. "That's Greig's Concerto in A minor" she said, without hesitation. I turned back to that station and there it was. I could not possibly have done that, even with music I know very well. It is partly a good musical memory, of course, but acute hearing must play its part.

Two further logical factors develop from this hearing lack. It becomes very nearly impossible to assess the quality of the music, to criticise the playing, the conducting; to tell the subtle differences between good choral singing and bad, between good phrasing and indifferent. Secondly, a musical note is not just a pure tone of say, 256 cycles per second. It contains within it a whole series of over-tones which may be very faint and barely perceptible but it is the presence of these harmonics which gives the note its characteristic quality and tells whether it is a flute, violin, trumpet and so on. An oboe, trumpet and cor anglais are instruments which a normal educated year can tell apart. Apart from the degree of loudness, I should find it difficult to distinguish between them and everything being equal, I hestitate to say that I could, in fact, do so.

You must therefore understand that listening to an orchestral concert is to me, a conglomeration of sounds from a number of instruments between which I cannot readily distinguish. "How dull!" says the acute listener and he is, alas, correct. It is like a colour-blind person gazing at a beautiful picture and trying to appreciate the glowing colours which to him are more or less varying shades of grey at its worst and a sadly depleted colour scheme at its best.

The church organ is my favourite instrument and precisely the same principles apply. First, I cannot appreciate the true tone of the organ since the higher harmonies are beyond me. Secondly, the effect of using the higher-pitched stops is precisely nil. Thirdly, due to the loss of the critical aural ability, it becomes impossible to assess the quality of an organ note or of an organ. They all tend to sound much alike except that some rumble more than others, since the pedal organ with its sub-unison tones affects me most. And of course it is very hard to follow the music.

The effect of wearing a hearing aid was to transform the situation entirely. Upon the acquisition of my first aid at the age of 29, it immediately became obvious that my capacity for hearing higher-pitched sounds was merely dulled and not entirely absent, as I had supposed. (This includes things like bird song). The effect of the hearing aid on musical notes was so devastating that I was unable to cope with it! The tone of an organ was so far removed from my life-long experience that it now sounded like a completely different instrument.

Ideally I should constantly have worn my new aid and re-educated my ears to the new experience, casting aside all thoughts of the old hearing and learning, as it were, a new musical language. It is to be regretted that I either funked it or was too lazy. It is not easy to adapt oneself, which is why older folk find it hard to grow accustomed to using an aid.

Besides, I did not need to wear it for everyday life. I need not have used it at all, used it only when necessary, or all the time — the choice we all have to make — and I elected to take the middle course.

However, after staggering along for some years and discarding my aid in church only because it made everything sound so strange, I finally had to pick up my cues from the rector. Thereafter, being obliged to grow accustomed to the new level of hearing, I wore it to concerts and organ recitals with a huge gain to my enjoyment. Though, again, I should really concentrate on learning what the solo instruments sound like — similar to learning a foreign language. The hard initial work would be repaid by greater subsequent pleasure.

The question of how much my singing is affected by deafness interests me greatly, the two outstanding facts being that while I cannot sing in tune (or tell if someone else is doing so), yet I possess perfect pitch and can usually tell in which key a piece of music is written. If the organist transposes a hymn, chant or anthem to a lower or higher key I am immediately aware of the fact and have to make a definite conscious effort to sing in the new key — thinking in terms of the sharpened or flattened music.

But ask me to sing a piece by myself unaccompanied and I shall change key with every note. How much is due to hearing lack and how much is a characteristic of the brain, I do not know. Similar choral failings are found in people with good hearing, who can range from being completely tone-deaf to being unable to sing in tune with four-part harmony — or even in unison. On the whole I sing in tune with the rest of the choir, but continually have to tune my voice by listening to the other singers. It is very aggravating not being able to hang directly on to a note without listening to someone else. My hearing aid greatly improved things, I suppose because it brought the sound right into my ear, which is why I wonder how much of this defect is due to deafness.

In similar fashion, when the Canterbury cathedral organist, Dr. Wicks, gave me the freedom of the organ on two occasions, I had to play with my aid turned off. The pipes are a long way from the console and the resultant time-lag plus the echoes made me so muddled that I had to stop playing!

Deafness

Anyone with a disability is not considered to be normal by general society. Concerning deafness we all know it is equated with daftness. The danger is that one's friends, acquaintances and even family will adopt this slogan to some extent and you may come to consider yourself mentally to be below par.

As I mentioned in my public school experiences, most people thought I was slightly mad and never lost a chance of making me look silly. In the adult world this attitude is not so obvious but it still exists nonetheless and I encounter people happy to make me look a fool, often cackling with stupid laughter when I have obviously misheard what has been said.

This feeling of inferiority therefore engenders a "chip on the shoulder". Slights and insults are assumed when none were intended. It is too easy to fall into moods of self-pity, the "nobody loves me because I am deaf" syndrome.

It is very hard to rid oneself of this attitude; after sixty-one years of being deaf I still fall into the trap although a bit of thought will show that deafness is not always the cause. Mr. ABC did not write because he was ill in hospital: Miss XYZ forgot to answer your invitation to a picnic because her mother was dying and not because she considered you a deaf silly-billy and scarcely worth bothering about. To understand all is often (not always!) to forgive all. All right, there are people who react adversely to your deafness; accept this as a fact and avoid them. It is impossible to be friends with everyone.

How then, can the deaf throw off this feeling of inferiority? The answer is, I think, to do something really well. It can be your job or a hobby. For my part I did farming for some years after failing at medicine and it was a poor venture but (with hindsight) maybe I was an inferior farmer. I took up grass cutting, specialising in the maintenance of churchyards and I can say — I hope with due modesty — that I have been very successful. To carve out a career from scratch at something never before attempted by anyone and to be self-employed at it for twenty-eight years accrues a good level of competence. In writing about being deaf and forced to think in depth about its problems, I have come to realise that this competence at my job and also in the small ventures into journalism, bolsters up my ego and therefore makes the problems due to the lack of hearing easier to bear.

Coupled with being competent in some way I would rate a happy marriage as another prime factor in a contented life. My wife has been asked whether it is possible to enjoy a happy marriage while being married to a deaf man. The answer is Yes, a thousand times. My wife has a very clear voice for which I never needed an aid at all. I do not need a hearing aid when we are alone together, she hears the door bell ring, the telephone bell sounding. If she is out I have to keep my aid working — a great bore. Until recently my Dog-Mate, Griffon Nobby would warn me but alas! I've lost him, although after he was fourteen he became deafer than his master. An understanding and practical wife is a solid support, my extra pair of ears.

A tiresome drawback of nerve deafness is communicating with children, as mentioned earlier, whose higher pitched voices are very difficult to catch, even with a hearing aid. When my two boys and girl were young, I possessed no hearing aid (the Medresco given me when I was about twenty-eight was only used for special occasions). It was very hard to understand what they were saying; their everyday chatter to their mother was lost on me. They did try — when they thought about it — to include me in the conversation by raising their voices and addressing me directly but it was an effort for both sides. Usually I opted out and left it to my excellent wife, who later would relay the gist of what the children had been talking about. This sort of thing she had taken on when we were married in 1944, making sure I was not left in ignorance of anything of importance. I note, with secret amusement, that members of my immediate family keep a sharp eye on me when I am conversing with anyone; they seem to know by instinct when I have gone adrift and immediately butt in to put me right! The three things I rate most highly in the never ending battle with deafness are: a happy marriage, a sympathetic family and competence in my job.

Some experiences are very much harder for the deaf, depending on the hearing loss. General conversation among a group of people is very difficult; many of us have given up trying to follow the speakers. My wife and I are bell-ringers in our small church. There is always conversation in the resting periods and I find it absolutely impossible to catch anything. In fact without my aid turned on I can only just hear the bells! It is much less exhausting to sit in silence; the others are aware of my problem — or should be — but I doubt if they realise just how lonely it makes me.

Listening to single speakers, as a lecturer giving a talk, is fairly straightforward as the aid can be accommodated to catch the speaker; questions from the floor will always be missed while explanatory remarks in a slide film show are also missed since it is not possible to lip-read in the darkness — and lip-reading will often make all the difference between hearing the speaker and actually understanding what he is saying.

Committee meetings are another trial and can be so exhausting as to lead to tension headaches. Speakers mumble and talk among themselves instead of addressing the Chair. I am not only a churchwarden but vice-chairman of the Church Council as well as being secretary. However, I flatly refused to attend to the minutes of the meetings and so we have a 'minute secretary' who does just that. An idea which could be copied by other committees anxious to acquire the services of a deaf person.

One final word of advice is offered to the recently deaf. Avoid the temptation of pretending your hearing is normal. Sooner or later you will fail and if people find you are giving silly answers or ignoring their greetings you'll be considered weak-minded or impolite, probably both.

You will find it necessary to keep reminding people you are deaf. They tend to forget and sometimes want to forget, to save themselves the bother of taking more care over their speech. If you miss what has been said to you, suggest it is phrased in different words, this often saves a lot of trouble. And it is an effort to take more care, make no mistake about it! Sometimes I encounter deaf customers and they can be extremely irritating, especially when they will not wear a hearing aid. It saves time and temper to ascertain just what sort of speech they best respond to — this is not necessarily shouting, which on the whole is of little use. I do not think there is much excuse for trying to manage without a hearing aid nowadays; it makes life so much easier, not only for the deafened but for those who have to deal with them. We are in a minority, living in a hearing world and we should try and make life tolerable for all. As I have written more than once, it is far better to explain you have a hearing problem and invite the speaker's co-operation which is generally forthcoming. Now I am older, when I meet a few people who try to take a rise out of me I tell them firmly — even rudely! — that they are very lucky not to have the same problems and they must hope it never happens to them.

My nerve deafness makes it difficult to hear sounds of higher pitch and therefore vowel sounds are easily missed. Speech can be loud enough to hear and yet the speaker might be speaking Sanskrit or Hindustani for all the sense I can make of his words. Of course, in such a situation I tend to cheat and pretend I have heard but as I said earlier, sooner or later one gets found out and made to look foolish; it really is not worth the effort and it is far better to explain your predicament. There are some people with quiet voices who seem incapable of making a sustained effort to make you hear them. Turning up your hearing aid is all right, provided there are not other speakers with much louder voices who will deafen you!

In my early churchyarding days I used to travel past the workhouse near Folkestone and tramps would wait outside in the early morning to cadge a lift towards Canterbury. I once picked up an Irishman who never stopped talking for the whole twenty minute ride. Not only did he possess a cleft palate but he seemed to be carrying a large hot potato in his mouth. I could follow about one word in ten of his conversation.

Generally I could pick out a key word or two and make a suitable rejoinder, like this: "Yehroo babry merthron hoohaa broken leg grogling hospital". "Oh really, was it very painful?" I'd answer. "I guston fiddledee six weeks glockwaa". I gathered he was telling me about the time his wife had three epileptic fits in bed one night, threw him out during the third fit and broke his ankle. Or maybe I got it wrong and he was really telling me about his dear old auntie in Tipperary.

While my speech is reasonably clear, some people find it hard to understand me. I tend to mispronounce some words — thus, until I was fourteen I said 'apologetic' instead of apoplectic. At the age of fifty I found that 'mansoleum' was not the pronounciation for mausoleum.

It is difficult for hearing people to put themselves in a deaf person's place — to think deaf. I was with an employer recently who was showing me a machine he thought a deaf person could not operate. "At a critical stage in the operation the buzzing noise stops" he said, "And the deaf man would not know when to go on to the next process". I had been watching the machine closely and pointed out that a light came on when the buzzing stopped. The employer, experienced though he was, was thinking as a hearing person. Even in this straightforward matter, with the light in front of him, he had been so busy hearing that he had not noticed the visual aid.

Hearing people cannot be blamed for not understanding deaf people. Those who use the sign language are a very small minority of the population, and most people go through life without meeting them. Their needs must be met, and the services should be provided as of right.

Deaf people lead relatively normal lives in that they are able to work, marry, have children and manage their own lives. But this seeming integration is superficial, and there are numerous services which should be either interpreted or specially presented if deaf people are to be able to lead full lives. This is not because deaf people are stupid or incapable, simply that they cannot hear.

One of the worst consequences of deafness is mental apathy, so if these services are not provided there is unlikely to be a great outcry from deaf people themselves.

All of us who suffer a series of accidents, bad luck, losing a job, illness or death in the family, ask at one stage or another: 'Why does this happen to me?' Probably we have led what we regard as blameless lives, done all that is expected of us, perhaps kept up a regular church attendance for many years, given to charity. And yet the queries persist. "Why does God treat me like this? What have I done to deserve it? He is supposed to be a 'loving Father' with the welfare of each one of us at heart; so why do I suffer this illness, painful affliction, disability ...?" and so on.

This sort of complaint comes with special frequency from those born with a disability of some sort — whether physical or mental — which is carried as a burden for a life-time. I, of course, think especially of deafness.

Deaf people cannot avoid some measure of frustration and bitterness. I as much as anyone, with perhaps rather more hearing than many, face the problem of listening to people, missing conversations, missing the full beauty of music, the song of birds ... Curiously, as a boy it did not worry me very much. It was not until I became a medical student that its impact on my future career first struck me.

I fear the Church of England, of which I am a member, has not the answer to my problem as to why I am deaf. Nor, indeed, has the Roman Catholic Church or any other conventional religious group. It is only because my interest in spiritual matters extends beyond the somewhat narrow bounds of conventional Christianity that I have found some measure of comfort in other spiritual points of view. It is because my thinking has helped me bear the burden of being deaf that I venture to pass it on to you.

For a start, take this idea of a 'Loving God' who wishes all his children to be 'happy'. I feel certain that while each one of us is cherished by spiritual powers, the 'loving' is not love as we commonly term it. C.S. Lewis in his 'Mere Christianity' describes it very well and I did not know what Christianity was really all about until I read this book. He points out that 'love', in this context, implies what is best for any soul but — and this is really the crux of the matter — what we think must be good for us in this life may not be what is ultimately good for our souls. The Almighty is looking at us with very long term prospects indeed!

So often we can look back on our lives and see a thread of purpose running through them. So many things may happen to us, utterly devastating at the time, grinding us down to the ground and yet providing an opportunity for future advancement or happiness. If we consider our lives as a sort of tapestry being woven by our thoughts and actions through a lifetime, it is obvious that we can only see the reverse side. The real design cannot be seen or understood by us in this life. Later, perhaps, we may exclaim: "Ah! Now that I can the proper pattern, I can understand why those things had to happen".

I look back on my own life — public school to Middlesex Hospital Medical School, the prospect of taking over my father's dental surgery practice in London's West End. Giving it all up at the age of twenty. Becoming a farm pupil in 1940, a farm worker, then having my own farm — which we had to leave when I was thirty-three, with heavy debts leaving me with no home, no other training and with a wife and three children. Yet out of that disaster came my churchyarding business and even in the darkest hours we always had a home and enough on which to live. Unexpected money came, for instance, once when I was particularly hard up, a neighbour offered to buy my flower pots, which were worth ten shillings. When I looked at his cheque I saw it was for a hundred pounds …

Since those days I have learnt a sense of being 'looked after', that there is no need to worry overmuch about tomorrow (although of course one has to do the day-to-day planning). Grass-cutting is seasonal and one might expect little work in the winter months; yet there has always been work without the need for advertising. I have learnt that even when the work available looks like running out in the following week, the Almighty always has something up his sleeve which he will reveal in his own good time and that there is no need for me to force the issue.

Many of you will be doing your best with what hearing you have and probably complaining about it. You will say that it is not fair, as I did. Why then have I changed my mind?

Because I have come more and more to believe that we are not born only once and then either go to Heaven — or get snuffed out like a candle! We are here to learn our lessons in a hard school; this life is a sort of academy and for many people an infernally hard and miserable one. Until we learn our lessons we make no progress. I suspect that when we leave this life we shall have to look back on what we have done, and have left undone, and how we must learn what was missed before, to strive towards perfection. To learn certain lessons we may need to undergo certain experiences and will be born again with certain kinds of bodies and to face situations to give us a chance of learning lessons which could not be learnt in any other way. After all, to put it another way, if you required a knowledge of farming then you would take a job on a farm, wouldn't you? Our bodies are but the agents for our real selves in the spiritual world — physical go-betweens — and it can truly be said that what we are sowing now, we will harvest in due course.

Those who cannot accept the reincarnation beliefs could still accept the general thesis; that this life is a preparation for what is to follow, that a lack of progress now means a set-back in the hereafter — whether this is to be a return here to earth or an existence in some other dimension. And everything we know here has its counterpart in the spiritual life — in fact everything had its origins in the spirit life first and not, as we like to think, here first with a sort of pale copy in the hereafter.

There is that passage in Luke, chapter seventeen, about servants and how if you do only what is expected of you then there is no particular merit gained. In fact the greater the gifts with which you have been endowed, the greater the advancement which will be expected of you! How much greater, in contrast, are the achievements of those who started with very little and yet manage much? Think of Helen Keller and of the governess inspired to teach her. Helen Keller did not just lead a normal life (I mean normal by her disabilities) but went on to become a great teacher and an inspiration to many. To her from whom so little could have been expected, how much must finally have been given! Could one not wonder if she had been sent into this life in that state in order to learn and that her governess had also been ordained in advance?

Of course I am painfully aware that this doctrine leaves many knotty problems unsolved. Evil perpetuated upon innocent victims in concentration camps or the sadism of kidnappers and bombers is hard to understand. But as I said, we see only one side of the tapestry and we cannot possibly see the real thing. Without knowing all the facts about tormentors and victims, perhaps stretching far back into history, we may not judge.

I believe therefore that I have been born deaf for some purpose and it is for me to make the best use of my time as a deaf person. Anyway, I think of my excellent fortunes — good health, a good wife, a happy home, enough money to live on, three grown-up and happy children (one who qualified as the doctor I never became), and a worthwhile job of service to the community. Really, it would appear that this came about through the handicap of my deafness, which thereby proves to be a blessing.